EXPLORING

FACTS

EXTRAORDINARY STORIES & WEIRD FACTS
FROM HISTORY TRIVIA BOOK

Exploring Facts

Extraordinary Stories & Weird Facts from History
Trivia Book

by Henry Bennett

illustrated by Bhanu Prakash Kushwaha

Liberstax Publishing

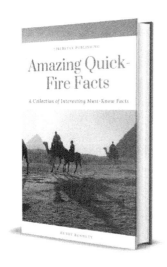

To help you along your investing in knowledge journey, we've provided a free and exclusive copy of the short book, *Amazing Quick-Fire Facts,* and a bonus copy of book, *The Big Book of Fun Riddles & Jokes*.

We highly recommend you sign up now to get the most out of these books. You can do that by visiting https://www.subscribepage.com/henrybennett to receive your FREE copies!

CONTENTS

Your New Trivia Quiz Blueprint!

There are so many trivia books out there, and most of them regurgitate the same stories over and over again. For example, everyone knows about the Titanic, the mystery and conspiracy theories surrounding The Bermuda Triangle, and even the conspiracy theory of D.B. Cooper. But surely there has to be more stories like these, stories few people know about but ones that are definitely worth mentioning and hypothesizing about!

This is where this book comes in with a list of lesser-known stories, facts, and trivia that will blow your mind. Many hours of painstaking research—listening to stories, conducting interviews—and referencing have gone into this book to produce a masterpiece that is different from others! To cater to the never-satisfied quiz and trivia nuts, a book was born that rehashes some of history's most fascinating tales that deserve a place in black and white—to be immortalized forever.

This journey will take you to many places, and you're guaranteed to be amazed at the results. For example:

- Did you know that a 25-year-old Roman nobleman named Julius Caesar was once captured by a band of Cicilian Pirates in the Aegean Sea?

- How a war was started because of an old, unimportant oak pail (at the time).

- Have you ever heard about the CIA's many failed attempts at killing off Fidel Castro?

- Bet you didn't know about the Italian spider dance that was once a cure but is now used as a flirty dance during special occasions.

- Find out more about the London-based actress who fell in love with an alien!

- Your mind will be blown by the many famous people whose brains have gone missing posthumously.

- And do you know the story of the most "kissed" girl in the world?

One thing is for sure, this collection of crazy stories and facts will have you rereading the book over and over again and impressing your friends with your newfound knowledge. Who doesn't like bragging rights?

These facts and tales range from true accounts of the paranormal to fan-based conspiracy theories that seem plausible in their own right and make you rethink everything you thought you knew about them.

Strap in and get ready to go on the journey of a lifetime as you explore the very best of the crazy stories that the world around us has on offer to those who open their minds!

The Most Fleeting War in History

Much can be said for how wars have globally shaped our futures, with some of them painfully lasting for years and leaving devastation in their wake. But did you know that the shortest recorded war in history is a little-known conflict called the Anglo-Zanzibar War? So, what makes this a crazy story? Well, it lasted no longer than 44 minutes. Yes, read that again! Can this even be called a war?

Enter 1896, when this briefest of conflicts started at 9:02 a.m. and ended at 9:46 that same morning, on the 27th of August. It all started as the result of a disagreement between Britain and the Sultanate of Zanzibar over who should succeed as predecessor after the passing of the last sultan.

As part of the agreement between the governments, under the rule of the British Protectorate, the British had to approve any successor to the Sultanate. However, the Zanzibaris broke this agreement when they disapproved of the new sultan Khalid bin Bargash.

The Britons retaliated by giving Zanzibar an ultimatum that expired on the 27th August 1896 at precisely 9:00 a.m. With the expiration date of the ultimatum passing, the new sultan went into hiding in the barricaded palace with his royal posse.

That day, 150 Royal Marines, two gunboats, and three cruisers entered the Zanzibari port in conjunction with 900 Zanzibar "traitors" who chose to join forces with the British Army. The sultan's palace was surrounded and bombarded at exactly 09:02, setting the castle on fire and defeating the Zanzibari Royal defense artillery. Finally, the flag was shot down and, with a deafening silence, all fire ceased.

After defeating the army of the unwanted sultan, Britain installed an approved sultan puppet ruler (one who owns a title indicating power but is, in fact, controlled by external forces and individuals), and they ruled for 67 years.

In its aftermath, the "war" left a 500-count casualty of Zanzibaris and only one Briton.

E.T.'s Earthly Burial

Legend has it that on September 22, 1983, a total of 13 trucks were driven to a secret location in Alamogordo, New Mexico. Their destination? A landfill, under the cover of darkness. The story goes that the contents of the trucks were dumped in the landfill, buried, and finally cemented, never to see the light of day again.

Apparently, a few days later (how, exactly, is unclear), word got out. Some scavengers went rummaging at the landfill and probably noticed the new addition at the dumpsite. Their find was none other than millions of copies of Atari's failed video game, *E.T.*, which was released the previous December in conjunction with the hit movie by Steven Spielberg.

Rumor has it that the botched attempt at an *E.T.* video game was the undoing of Atari and caused the company's downfall. As for the video games, it's said they were buried to hide Atari's shame.

In April 2014, after being fascinated with the story for years, a renowned writer of the Marvel franchise, Zak Penn, deployed an excavation crew to exhume the site. One of the many interesting facts he uncovered was that the game's creator, Howard Scott Warshaw (dubbed Atari's rockstar at the time), was charged with producing the game but only had a mere five months to put it together and out on the market. This is strange as when Spielberg commissioned him to produce a similar video game product for *Raiders of the Lost Ark* as a tie-in to the movie, he had a more reasonable 10 months to get the job done.

On the day of the planned excavation, *E.T.* fans gathered around the site. Not long after, they weren't disappointed when the first *E.T.* video game cartridge was unearthed—a moment that left Warshaw in tears.

The conclusion? The fable was half-true, as Penn and his crew managed to find 1,300 unloved and buried *E.T.* video game cartridges unsold and intact. Even more strange is the fact that the dumpsite was not far from Atari's California headquarters at the time.

Sidenote: Why does New Mexico seem to be the global hub for everything extraterrestrial-related? #askingforafriend

Good Ole King Tut—The "Boy King"

Now, some of you might be familiar with the story of King Tutankhamun, but the following facts below will blow your mind!

1. His birth name was not Tutankhamun

His birth name was actually "Tutankhaten." His birth name reflects his parents' adoration for the sun god named "the Aten," and Tutankhaten means "living image of the Aten" when translated. Upon his early (some say premature) ascension to the throne at the tender age of nine, the new pharaoh abandoned his house religion and turned to the King of the God's following by electing to worship the god Amun instead. This saw him change his identity to that of Tutankhamun, which means "living image of Amun"—the name we've come to know him by.

2. King Tut has the smallest tomb in the Valley of the Kings

Initially, it was fashionable in pre-1550 BC for any expired pharaohs to be buried in elaborate pyramids in the northern part of the Egyptian desert. But with the rise of the New Kingdom (1550–1069 BC), fallen kings were buried in secrecy in their final resting place, now known as the Valley of the Kings, located on the western bank of the Nile river.

Even though the doors were less obvious, it's said the tombs are spacious inside and opulently decorated, fit for a king.

Sadly, despite what Tutankhamun might've wanted, it is known that he was buried in a compact tomb in the floor of the main western valley and not with his grandfather, Pharaoh Amenhotep III, in the northern part of the desert.

The exact reason why seems to be unknown. Was it because King Tut died so young and had not fulfilled his obligations? Or is it due to the fact that his royal tomb was incomplete at the time of his death? Certain Egyptologists believe there are secret compartments hidden in his underwhelming tomb, and they're currently investigating the possibility of undergoing deeper delving.

3. He was buried in a second-hand sarcophagus

As if the previous fact wasn't questionable enough, the young king is also said to be buried in a hand-me-down coffin. Historically, pharaohs had been buried in a set of three golden coffins that fit neatly into one another—much like a Russian nesting doll effect.

Upon Tutankhamun being laid to rest, the funeral staff found that the outer coffin was too big for the boy king, and the royal carpenters were tasked to saw off the toes of the casket as it was unable to close. Circa 3,000 years later, British archeologist Howard Carter made the discovery of a lifetime when he found these coffin fragments in the base of King Tut's sarcophagus.

4.   **Tutankhamun's heart is AWOL**

The ancient Egyptians were firm believers that one can be reincarnated in the afterlife—providing that your last vessel (body) was preserved in a life-like condition for the next journey. This saw the birth of the concept of mummification.

Mummification implied that the fallen pharaoh's internal organs were to be removed and preserved separately from the body. By that time (due to lack of science and understanding), the brain was discarded from the corpse. However, the heart is said to have been seen as the organ of reasoning by the Egyptians at the time and was left with the body. If it was found to be taken out, it was quickly returned to the body— albeit not being sewed in at its place of origin.

However, in King Tut's case, he was found heartless, with an amulet in the shape of a scarab (insect) inscribed with a funerary spell. But why? Is it because the undertakers were careless? Or is it because the young pharaoh died so far away from home that by the time he reached his home, his heart was too decayed or even missing for it to be preserved?

The Puritans Canceled Christmas in 1659

When the devout Puritans sailed from the shores of England to Massachusetts in 1620, it is said that they brought a surprising concept with them to the United States—an utter distaste for Christmas! So, instead of a scene filled with Christmas music, lights, fanfare, and that magical feeling associated with the holiday, these pious individuals forced their staff to work and kept their churches' doors firmly shut.

After beheading the English king Charles I in 1647, their next order of business was to effectively cancel Christmas and everything it stood for, as we have come to celebrate it in modern times. Instead, the 25th of December was declared a day of humiliation and fasting for Englishmen to atone for their sins incurred the other 364 days of the year. It seems like a hefty price to pay on a day that is earmarked for celebration, appreciation, rest, and family union in the Christian religion! To make matters worse, if you were caught doing anything other than "making amends," you were slapped with a five-shilling fine.

But why did the Puritans detest Christmas so much in particular? Well, firstly, this is due to their theological beliefs, and secondly, they hated the fanfare surrounding the holiday in the 1600s. Their interpretation of the bible was that there were no grounds for celebrating the arrival and birth of Jesus Christ for one day, let alone an entire festive season as we call it today.

The Puritans also believed that the celebration of Christmas is attached to pagan roots. This is largely because Rome only declared an official nativity celebration on December 25 after the 4th century BC. Naturally, this made the Puritans feel that more sinning occurred during the 12 days of Christmas than the rest of the calendar year.

So, when did the change come about for the inhabitants of Massachusetts? The first steps to the public's acceptance of Christmas celebrations weren't until 1685, when the newly-appointed governor, Sir Edmund Andros, attended church, sang hymns, and was spotted praying—all the while under the guard of his protection detail. But it was 1856 before Christmas was turned back into a public (bank) holiday, and celebrations returned to normal. You simply can't make stuff like this up!

Was William Shakespeare a Fraud?

With any famous person, you will always find controversy and mystery surrounding them. This all comes down to the fact that the more popular they are, the more we as humans elevate them to a god-like status. So much so, we don't think about the fact that they are ordinary people, too, because this thought simply doesn't track with their extraordinary achievements, lives, and statuses.

One bard, William Shakespeare, is no stranger to conspiracy. When we hear his name, we are transported to a different era, awash with romantic and intense protagonists and antagonists. So, let's delve into some facts and evidence that we *do* know.

Firstly, most of Shakespeare's family is said to be poor and illiterate—there is no factual evidence that verifies that he was even educated enough to write. He did questionable things like writing his own name differently on each manuscript and play; other historical figures mostly referred to him as an actor and not a writer; and lastly, when he passed, there was no mention of any of the works associated with him in his will and testament—add that to the fact that the will wasn't penned in his usual poetic writing style. Mind-blowing, right?

Some believe that Sir Francis Bacon was behind the works because while William was born poor, for some uncanny reason, he could write about the nobles and their opulent lifestyles in great detail—how can you write about a topic you have no intimate knowledge about? On top of that, when Bacon and Shakespeare's works are compared, there are a lot of similarities that one simply can't ignore.

Another theory fantasized by conspiracy theorists is that a group of ghostwriters were responsible for the many works that Shakespeare is credited for. Why? This is due to the presence of a group of writers called the Oxford Syndicate during the same period, and the fact that Shakespeare was never seen writing alone. So, was Shakespeare even a genuine person?

Fact or fiction? You decide!

The Einstein President-Elect DENIED!

Most of you are undoubtedly well-versed with Albert Einstein's place in the scientific community and the fact that he is credited as being one of the most brilliant human minds in history. But very few people know that Einstein was offered the Israeli presidency—but declined.

That's right! On top of the many contributions that Albert brought to the world of physics, he was also a keen political activist. He was an advocate for eradicating crimes against humanity such as Nazism and racism but never had the support of politicians in this regard due to their ignorance of these critical matters.

The hardships that Einstein and his people endured before and after the Second World War had affected him profoundly, and subsequently, this saw him champion the aforementioned causes. Moreover, as a Jew, he stood up for the rights of his community and Israel in particular.

On November 16, 1952, then Prime Minister David Ben Gurion wrote a letter to his acquaintance Abba Edn, the head of the Israeli embassy, and requested that he approach the "greatest Jew on Earth"—a.k.a Einstein—and ask if he would consider accepting the role of Israel's new president. This would imply that the physicist would have to immigrate to

Israel immediately and obtain citizenship to become eligible for the role of commander-in-chief.

Edn agreed and penned a letter to Einstein. Two days later, on November 18, Albert responded with a letter of his own—in which he politely declined the offer and stated several reasons behind his refusal of this coveted position.

His exact response was: *"I am deeply moved by the offer of our state Israel and at the same time sad and ashamed because I cannot accept it. All my life, I have had to deal with objective things, so I lack both the natural ability and the experience of doing well with people and exercising official duties. Given these reasons alone, I should be inadequate to fulfill the official duties, even if my old age would not regain my power. I am even more saddened by these circumstances as my relationship with the Jewish people has become the strongest human connection I have ever since I became fully aware of our precarious situation among the nations of the world."* (Offering the Presidency of Israel to Albert Einstein, 2019).

Even though this was Einstein's response, many wonder to this day if the real reason behind his polite refusal was because he didn't want to cause a territorial separation between the Arabs and the Jews. Additionally, he is said to have been a pacifist—meaning his views would be completely different than the flock he was invited to lead.

Wojtek—The WWII Polish Soldier Bear

Animals have cemented themselves as heroes since time immemorial. But when you travel to Poland, they have a unique animal war-hero story to tell—one of a 600-pound, beer-drinking, cigarette-smoking brown bear called Wojtek.

On April 8, 1942, a group of Polish POWs (Prisoners of War) discovered a little bear cub in the Iranian mountain range. They took the cub with them and bottle-fed it using a mixture of condensed milk and vodka. As with any baby animal, though, Wojtek eventually grew up.

One of the surviving POWs fondly recounted how Wojtek would light and puff on a smoke before swallowing it. To add to the horror of animal rights advocates is the fact that the bear was also a keen beer lover and would be seen chugging down a whole bottle and then forlornly peeking into the empty neck to see where the rest of the beer was, much to the delight of his caregivers.

Amongst Wojtek's many shenanigans, he learned how to turn on the shower by himself in the pursuit of a cold drink, resulting in the men missing their rations of water amid shortages. It's said that the bear appeared to enjoy play and fetch sessions by running after the oranges the men used for grenade practice.

The animal earned his keep by holding new recruits upside down by their boots in a bid to scare them as part of the initiation process. At one time, Wojtek was apparently seen carrying live ammo and loading guns. This saw him obtain both a ranking and a number like any other enlisted soldier.

After WWII ended and the Polish scattered in all directions, the fate of Wojtek was in jeopardy. The POWs didn't want the bear to return to Poland as they feared it would be seen as a symbol of communism (the exact thing they fought against). Luckily, Wojtek found a new home in the rolling hills of Scotland when he was relocated farm side amongst other Polish fighters stationed there post-war.

He became a much-loved performance pet for all who lived there until his passing in 1963 due to esophageal damage— could this have been a result of his cigarette-swallowing habit? Nevertheless, you can view a bronze statue erected in his honor in central Edinburgh in 2015.

Count Dracula Was Real!

The first book written about Count Dracula was released on May 26, 1897, penned by Irish writer Bram Stoker. Unlike the fictional story of the Cullen clan in the *Twilight* saga, this "bloodsucker" was real.

In true fashion, some believe that the real Count Dracula (Vlad the Impaler) was born in modern-day Romania, which was then known as none other than Transylvania. However, this is a highly contentious debate as some scholars say the real prince never had any affiliation to Transylvania whatsoever.

He might've not been washed in a golden glow when sunlight kissed his skin, and the medieval prince Vlad the Impaler was said not to be a clinical vampirism practitioner who "suffered" from Renfield's syndrome, an obsession with consuming human blood. Still, he was apparently the inspiration behind all Count Dracula-related novels.

But if he wasn't a blood drinker, why is he branded as Count Dracula? The name "Dracula" was bestowed on him as a result of his horrific, draconian, and cruel style of punishment against his enemies. The name is derived from the old Romanian word for "dragon." Stoker is also said to have made use of the word for "devil" in Wallachian and brought them together to form the concept of Count Dracula as a result of the devilish actions of Vlad.

Unlike Stoker's character, Vlad did not receive an immortal status. Instead, he met his demise in 1476 when the Ottomans ambushed and killed his army. The only thing that remains today are the tales of Vlad's tyranny and how his victims had to die in fear when realizing their cruel fate—something that haunts modern society to this very day.

Cleopatra Was NOT Egyptian

There are many interesting facts that surround this fabled Queen of the Nile:

She was more Macedonian-Greek than Egyptian

Yes, she was born in Egypt, but her roots can be traced back all the way to Macedonian Greece and one of Alexander the Great's generals, Ptolemy I. Even though the general ruled Egypt, he created a dynasty of rulers that conversed in Greek. Cleopatra adopted many Macedonian-Greek customs and was the first of the Ptolemy line that spoke Egyptian.

She was born of incest

It's no secret that royal dynasties worldwide married their cousins and siblings to preserve the purity of the bloodline, and it is said that Cleopatra is the product of a union between brother and sister. She kept up with tradition and married two of her own brothers, who served by her side during her reign.

Cleopatra led a fleet in battle

Rumor has it that Cleo's greatest asset was, in fact, not her beauty but rather being well-schooled in the art of seduction— so much so that she managed to seduce her then-husband Roman general Mark Anthony's bitter archrival, Octavian.

This saw Octavian branded with a capital *T*, for traitor! As a result, the Roman Senate declared war on Cleopatra.

Side-by-side, Cleopatra and Anthony bravely fought with their fleet of naval ships against their shared archenemy. Sadly, they failed, and this saw them both flee to Egypt to avoid capture.

Cleo and Anthony had a drinking club

Known as a couple who adored each other's company, the pair formed their own drinking club called the "Imitable Livers"— I can't help but wonder if this name is a result of them living a life of leisure and luxury in the winter of 41–40 BC, or whether they also had a keen sense of humor and might've invented the first pun, too. The reason I say so is that this leisurely lifestyle saw them consuming copious amounts of alcohol during this time. Moreover, all the feasting and drinking saw them play host for many parties and soirees that included pranks and party games with the community's residents.

Fidel Castro and the Exploding Cigar

One of the many rumored failed assassination attempts from the Central Intelligence Agency (CIA) in the US has to be that of Cuban revolutionary Fidel Castro in 1961. The CIA took a box of his favorite cigars and laced each one with botulinum toxin, potent enough to kill anyone who attempts to put the cigar in their mouth.

A year after Castro came into power the box of explosive contraband is said to have been delivered to an unidentified person who was to hand them to "El Commandante." Needless to say that the "present" never reached Fidel, and to this day, it's a mystery as to what exactly happened to the box. It must be a curious case of "close but no cigar"?

You might be surprised to learn that this was only one of more than 634 creative, but ambitious attempts to rid the earth of Castro. One other attempt involved turning one of his lovers against him by arming her with a series of CIA-issued poison pills. As the pills started to melt away, she realized that she had to all but force them down the Cuban's throat. Apparently, Fidel guessed the plot and went as far as handing her his own pistol and telling her to take the shot, but she was unable to. So, does the fact that Castro managed to outfox the CIA for half a century make him their most ardent adversary?

Fidel Castro finally died of natural causes at the ripe old age of 90 on November 25, 2016.

Everything is Big in Japan!

Okay, maybe not *everything* is "big in Japan," but the country is home to the world's busiest train station: Shinjuku station. This transport hub, the brainchild of architect Junzo Sakakura was constructed in 1885. It also once served as a stop along the Koshu-Kaido highway heading West. It's steeped in history, as it's said that the ancient Samurai warriors didn't sleep too far away from the station.

During the Edo period (1600–1867), the Naito clan held the area, and it's believed that this post-war shin (station) could tell many a tale of the Samurai lords and their retainers passing through from the shogun's castle. In those days, Shinjuku was the first stop on their foot travels.

Modernization came into play in Tokyo in the 1860s, and with it, the first railway in 1872. As time went by, three new additional lines were added: the Chuo line, the Keio line, and the Odakyu line. Later, all of the lines became the Yamanote loop line—the most famous in the country.

Today, Shinjuku station sees a whopping total of 3.64 million passengers traveling through its doors daily, making it the world's busiest station—an accolade obtained in 2011 from the Guinness World Records. The station now comprises five satellite stations, more than 50 platforms, and in excess of 200 exits said to be operational from 4:30 a.m. to 1:00 a.m. the next morning.

Caesar and the Cilician Pirates—*Arrrrrr!*

At the age of 25, Julius Caesar was sailing the Aegean Sea when he was captured by Cilician pirates. The works of the famous author and Greek biographer Plutarch details that Caesar was kidnapped and held for a ransom of 20 silver talents ($600,000 in today's value). At the time, the pirates had no idea of the value of their prisoner, as his identity to them was unclear. Julius was apparently extremely offended at the suggestion of the meager amount and implored them to ask for 50 talents instead ($1,400,116,57 today).

The Cilician pirates eagerly agreed, and this saw Caesar send his associates off to gather the ransom—a feat that apparently took 38 days in total. It also appears that Julius had no qualms in remaining with the pirates and was seen ordering them around and treating them like they were beneath him. One of the things he demanded was for them to remain quiet when he slept. Apparently, the pirates enjoyed the discipline as Julius was free to pretty much come and go as he pleased on the pirate fleet and islands, and he was even seen writing poetry with them.

It seems Julius Caesar was experiencing a bit of Stockholm syndrome by growing close to his captors, but he made it abundantly clear that he did not appreciate being held there against his will. Caesar went so far as to tell them that once he was freed, he would crucify them for holding him captive.

Once the ransom was paid and he regained his freedom, he did exactly as he promised. Although he was deemed a private citizen, he assembled a fleet and returned to the pirate island. He found them exactly where he left them as if they thought nothing much of his idle threats. Julius took back the 50 talents ransom, all the pirates' possessions, and the pirates themselves.

His captors were delivered to the Pergamon prison, and Caesar approached Marcus Junius (proconsul of Asia) with a petition to have the pirates executed by crucifixion. However, Junius declined Caesar's request—he wanted to sell the pirates as slaves and keep the money from the sales.

Julius returned to Pergamon and took matters into his own hands, making good on his promise of crucifying them. However, he cut their throats first as a sign of "mercy."

Planetary Death by Gas

So, before Halley's comet managed to avoid plummeting to Earth and killing us all via cyanogen gas, some superstitious individuals believe that it did, in fact, kill King Edward VII— it didn't. However, they still thought it did… somehow! This comet and the perceived apocalyptic-ish feel that came with it saw the British blaming it for the impending German invasion, while the French thought it the culprit behind the flooding of the Seine.

The comet's discoverer Edmond Halley predicted that the infamous (then nine-mile-long) comet would appear every 76 years, together with measurable amounts of anxiety. Somehow, in 1910, the panic was elevated to another level by fearmongers when Earth's inhabitants believed we would meet our demise when the deadly gas entered our hemisphere.

Naturally, on the lighter side, creatives and art producers alike cashed in on the so-called disaster in the making by breaking out in song and poetry, and the comet was even synonymized with a Pears soap commercial. "Medication manufacturers" added to the fear by developing what they termed as an "anti-comet pill."

Needless to say, the eagerly anticipated comet came and passed on May 19, 1910, and realizing that all and sundry survived, much dancing and delight ensued in the streets. If you are reading this book in 2061, prepare thyself—with sunglasses, at most!

The Phantom Ship—*Mary Celeste*

Initially dubbed the *Amazon*, the now-famous ghost ship is a tale shrouded in mystery. She was a 282-ton brigantine that set sail on the 7th of November, 1872, from New York to Italy. Onboard were eight crew members, the captain Benjamin Briggs, his wife, and their daughter. On December 5, the phantom ship was spotted by British vessel the *Dei Gratia* approximately 400 miles east toward the Azores in full self-sail but sans any humans.

The *Dei Gratia* crew boarded the empty vessel and found all humans and one lifeboat gone. They had left behind six months' worth of supplies and an undamaged ship barring the hold filled with several feet of water.

The *Mary Celeste* had an ominous connection from the beginning that included the unexplained and sudden illness and death of one captain and a collision with another ship. Eventually, after exchanging hands no less than 12 times, the last captain ran her to the ground in his bid to commit insurance fraud.

Captain Briggs' diary is said to have detailed that the trip was quite pleasant. However, the first investigators to undertake a fact-finding mission in the 19th century did uncover something quite peculiar—the merchant ship had 1,700 barrels of alcohol onboard at the time of its departure. Nine of the barrels were made from red oak wood and were empty. The rest, made from white oak wood, were found intact. Why is this curious? Because it's known that in those days, white oak barrels were waterproof, but red oak was porous. So, did the alcohol leak out of the red oak barrels and cause a panic amongst the crew, forcing them to retire to the liferaft? It might be, but to this day it doesn't explain why the rope that the lifeboat was attached to had been severed.

Another person who claimed to have found the *Mary Celeste* is none other than bestselling author Clive Cussler. He discovered a ship in 2011; however, upon closer examination, it was determined that the wreck he unearthed was at least a decade older than when the boat in question sank.

Many theories have since been hypothesized, such as the crew being devoured by a monster or taken hostage by savage pirates. It simply made no sense for a seasoned sailor such as the missing Captain Briggs to just abandon a perfectly good vessel.

The only thing we know for sure is that the last entry in the logbook was made on December 5, where the crew detailed being within sight of the Azore Islands. To this day, the fate of Briggs and his crew remains a mystery, and we'll probably never be the wiser.

Captain Morgan was a Real Person

Rum lovers worldwide are probably delighted at the fact that their brand hero did, in fact, exist. One Sir Henry Morgan was a 17th century Welsh privateer and an admiral in the Royal Navy. His day job? Raiding Spanish villages in the Caribbean. Brand creators Diageo loved their brand ambassador so much that they funded the excavation of one of Morgan's ships in 2011, when it was discovered just shy of the Panama coast. The commissioned diver Frederick Hanselmann uncovered a piece of Morgan's flagship, *Satisfaction*, and with it, boxes and other cargo believed to be part of the ruthless admiral's then-booty.

Hooked, are you? Here are some other fascinating Morgan-related facts:

Captain Morgan and the NFL

For a while, it was rumored that Diageo pledged to donate $10,000 to the Gridiron Greats fund every time a player scored a touchdown. This fund is responsible for the financial and medical well-being of retired players. However, in 2009, the NFL brought an abrupt end to players striking a Morgan pose because it was in direct contravention of its policies in players promoting commercial brands in their capacity.

Rum Morgan Rum

After Smirnoff vodka (also owned by Diageo), Captain Morgan rum is the second-best-selling spirit in its category, totaling a whopping 5.59 million nine-liter cases in 2020 alone (Statista 2020, n.d.).

Hick!

The Morgan rum variety with the highest volume of alcohol content is the "Black Cask" variety, which is 100 proof—meaning it comprises 50% alcohol by volume.

Vegan-friendly

El Capitan is said to even support the vegan folk. Not only is the product not made from any animal derivatives, Captain Morgan rum never has and will never be tested on animals—other than Homo sapiens.

The captain and dislocated hips

One ER doctor was inspired by a Captain Morgan advertisement that influenced the development of a new way to pop back a dislocated hip. Wowzer! Who knew? It appears there is much more to the Morgan pose than initially thought.

Ketchup for the Cure

Today, in our modernized society, tomato ketchup—or tomato sauce, as some countries like South Africa call it—has a variety of uses as a cleaning hack. But did you know that in the 1830s, our ancestors used ketchup for medicinal purposes? Founding father Dr. John Cook Bennett from Ohio went one step further to develop tomato pills that were used for a variety of ailments, such as jaundice, indigestion, and diarrhea, to name a few.

Singlehandedly, Bennett changed the public's view of tomatoes forever. You see, before his findings were made known, people used to believe tomatoes were poisonous. However, Bennett's concoction, made by boiling them down into ketchup form, made them take notice and change their minds.

Three years on, entrepreneur Archibald Miles capitalized on Bennett's invention by selling tomato ketchup as medicine and a condiment. While Miles had a devout following, he came under intense scrutiny from medical professionals. His products were found to be nothing more than gimmicks, apart from alleviating constipation.

Even though Miles' claims were rubbished, the tomato was never overlooked again. Today, some people believe these love apples to be a cancer preventer, amongst other magical properties—such as bringing life to even the blandest of sliders. Best of all? The tomato is regarded as the hero of the vegetable-loathing child (and adult) worldwide!

Bucket Wars

The War of the Bucket between two regions in Italy, Modena and Bologna, has to be one of the most ridiculous wars ever started. Why? Well, it's because blood was spilled over a wooden bucket. To make matters worse, said bucket didn't even bear any value or historical significance.

Legend goes that in 1325, a group of soldiers from Modena sneaked into Bologna and stole an oak bucket used to scoop water from a central well in the city's square. The only thing this act did was to hurt Bologna's pride, and they demanded that the wooden bucket be returned to its rightful place. Needless to say, Modena refused, and Bologna retaliated by declaring war on them—and that's how the Battle of Zappolino was started.

That day, Bologna deployed no less than 32,000 soldiers, but all that Modena could manage to scramble together were a meager 7,000 in response. Though Modena was severely outnumbered, they fought bravely. A few hours after the war was started, it was over, with Modena chasing Bologna back to their city gates in utter humiliation. Not only did they destroy numerous castles, but they also segregated Bologna from their main water source and orchestrated a faux athletic event called a *palio* as mockutainment—and, *just* before

Thrice now, Dorante-Day has failed in legal attempts to prove he is a royal. However, this didn't stop him. He is currently in the process of a fourth try to get someone to listen. It is said that he has submitted another round of paperwork to the Australian High Court, demanding that Prince Charles and Duchess Camilla submit to DNA testing.

Thailand's Monkey Buffet

It's always fun to go to a petting zoo, but sadly few people are afforded the opportunity to see uncaged wild animals dine. But if you find yourself in Thailand on the last Sunday in November, you can get up close with some macaque monkeys.

Nestled amongst the historic ruins of the Phra Prang Sam Yot temple in Lopburi, you can enjoy watching the primates indulge in a two-ton buffet of fruit and other ape-friendly culinary delights. To add to the atmosphere is a splendor of brightly dressed folk dancing in monkey costumes. Before the festivities start, the monkeys are sent invites to the party with a cashew nut attached. The dancers then lure the monkeys to the spread in song and dance, and then the buffet is revealed to the guests of honor. It is said that no less than 2,000 attend the festival annually, and a total of 20 chefs are employed to prepare the food and beverages for the animals.

The festival totals 500,000 baht ($15,000) each year, with 18,000 baht ($537,26) being spent on expensive durian alone. Durian is an edible, pungent fruit with custard-like flesh. Talk about laying it on thick!

The locals believe that the presence of the monkeys brings them good fortune as lady luck shines upon them. This uncanny respect for the macaques dates back circa 2,000 years ago when the divine Prince Rama struggled to rescue his wife from the stronghold of a demonic lord. Rama apparently enlisted the help of the monkey king Hanuman and his army, who defeated the king's enemy and rescued his beloved Sita. Since then, the monkey buffet of Lopburi has been used as an annual observance by Thailand to show their appreciation to Hanuman.

This has to be a bucket list item to do when you are in Thailand, but keep your bags and purses firmly stowed away to avoid any monkey business.

That Time When Pepsi Became a Military Power

What does it take to be recognized as a military power? Apparently nothing other than a significant number of weapons and fighting craft in your possession. But what happens when one of America's beverage giants becomes part of this equation... unexpectedly?

In 1959, then US President Eisenhower arranged an American National Exhibition in Moscow in a bid to promote American culture and products to the USSR (Russia, today). Shortly after the opening, it's said that Nixon and Soviet leader Krushchev got into loggerheads with one another. The heated argument caused much discomfort to the exhibition attendees, and the VP of Pepsi at the time, Donald Kendall, gave the Soviet leader a cup of Pepsi to take his attention away from the debate with Nixon.

Thanks to Kendall, Krushchev liked the beverage so much that he permitted its entry into the USSR, and it subsequently became the first American product to be consumed in the Soviet Union. Another lesser-known fact is that the argument was completely staged. You see, at the time, Pepsi wasn't keen on sending Kendall to the USSR, and he approached Nixon for his help in executing the brilliant idea—and it worked!

Even though it took another decade for the product to hit the Soviet shelves, America also got something out of the deal. Both stakeholders decided that the fairest trade option would be good old-fashioned bartering. So, the Soviets exchanged their prized Stolichnaya vodka for American-made Pepsi, and the rest is history, as they say.

The Soviet consumers responded very kindly to the new product—so much so that it eventually became a status symbol for those who drank it. By the end of the 80s, it was estimated that the USSR alone consumed a billion units of Pepsi annually!

In 1989, Pepsi realized that the American consumers didn't want as much of the Soviet vodka as the Soviets wanted of the cola-based beverage. They were bored and wanted a new deal. The Soviets, on the other hand, were very keen to keep the product and needed a way to compensate for the $3,000,000,000 in revenue Pepsi now brought into the USSR. Guess what the Soviets had in surplus! That's right—after the cold war, they had extra military equipment.

This saw the Soviets offer 17 submarines, a destroyer, a cruiser, and a frigate as a barter for the $3,000,000,000. Pepsi pondered on this and eagerly accepted the deal, making them the sixth-largest military power worldwide. Sadly, Pepsi now sat with a bunch of military vessels they had no use for, which resulted in them flogging the lot to a Swedish company that turned the equipment into scrap metal for recycling purposes. Ouch! What would've happened if Pepsi had kept their fleet and participated in the Gulf War against Iraq a year later?

Mercy Brown—New England's Last Vampire

In the 19th century, very little was known about tuberculosis. At the time, it was known as the consumption, and the disease all but literally consumed the inhabitants, making them do unthinkable acts against their families. The densely populated regions of New England at the time didn't help matters much, contributing to the ease with which the illness spread.

Because very little was understood about the disease at the time, it was only natural that many a conspiracy theory was birthed as a result. As with any pandemic, the disease spread from one family to another, causing the townspeople to succumb to death. The fact that no one could pinpoint the cause or a cure only added to the eeriness surrounding the disease—so much so that it was believed a recently deceased member would rise from the dead to drain the very life from those still breathing. This brought about the age of vampirism in the region.

One such family with a story to tell is the Browns. The mother, Mary Eliza Brown, was the first to die of the disease, and four years later, the eldest daughter Mary Olive succumbed at the tender age of 20. It was when the Browns' only son Edwin caught the disease that action was first taken. Despite taking matters into his own hands and receiving top medical care in Colorado, he returned home defeated as his condition further deteriorated. To make matters worse, his other sister Mercy sadly passed away while he was receiving treatment.

Edwin's father simply could not stand losing another family member to the dreaded disease—and so he began exhuming the bodies of his wife and his two deceased daughters. With the aid of the town's doctor, some neighbors, and the local paper, the three bodies were removed from their graves. It was found that Mary Eliza and Mary Olive's bodies were decaying as expected, but Mercy's body looked the same nine weeks later, and blood was also still present in her heart and liver. This brought about the suspicion that Mercy was busy draining the life out of Edwin, hence her blood being intact and Edwin's condition worsening.

Out of pure desperation, the Brown family resorted to extreme measures by removing Mercy's heart and liver. The organs were burned to ashes and fed to Edwin, but none of it helped, and he died. Unfortunately, their story is a sad tale with no happy ending as a decade later, Edwin's 19-year-old sister Mary Lena also succumbed to consumption.

If you're ever in the area, you can visit Mercy's final resting place behind the Baptist Church at The Chestnut Hill Cemetery in Exeter. Here, you can get a glimpse into New England's vampire panic in the 19th century.

Napoleon Under Siege From Bunnies!

Was Napoleon's bitter defeat Waterloo, or was it an event that occurred several years earlier? Because eight years before the Battle of Waterloo, the French emperor was overpowered by a colony of rabbits! Yes, you read right the first time!

As with any tale stranger than fiction, there are a few versions of the story. However, most historians agree that the event occurred after Napoleon signed the Treaties of Tilsit in July 1807. Apparently, in celebration of the document being signed, which signaled the end of the war between Imperial Russia and the French Empire, Napoleon suggested a rabbit-hunting excursion and ordered his chief of staff to make the arrangements.

The chief of staff made it happen—and in a big way. He collected many rabbit nests (some say a total of 3,000), arranged an outdoor lunch spread, and even invited some top military personnel. Once the hunters were ready, the bunnies were released from their cages, and chaos ensued.

Instead of the fluffy rodents running away in fright, they fought back by overwhelming Napoleon and his men. What was first perceived as a joke quickly turned serious when the bunnies couldn't be warded off with bullwhips, riding crops, or sticks as they continued to swarm the hunting party.

The defeated emperor fled the scene by returning to his carriage, but apparently, the ambush didn't stop there. The rabbits were said to have devised a cunning military plan of their own by splitting into two groups and attempting to surround the carriage, entering it from both flanks.

Eventually, the rabbits relinquished as they saw Napoleon and his hunting party speeding off in the field. Chief of Staff Berthier was blamed for the unfortunate incident, in which Napoleon's pride was undoubtedly hurt.

Ice Age Reincarnated?

There's no doubt that nature keeps on surprising us in ways we probably never thought possible. One such story takes us to Siberia, where Russian scientists made an interesting discovery: They found seeds of the *Silene stenophylla* plant. The catch? It's believed to date back 32,000 years (give or take 300-odd years, just for good measure).

Not only did they find the arctic plant, but they managed to resurrect it. The cache seeds were unearthed 124 ft below a thick subsurface layer of soil called permafrost. Then, to add to the curiosity factor, the seeds were found under the ice and revived using the glass vial method of growing.

The age-old question that scholars need to determine is how the seeds could survive up to now. Thanks to climate change, the ice is now melting, and it gives scientists the perfect opportunity to investigate the matter further. On the surface, it appears that the seeds of the plant with white flowers have an uncanny ability to adapt to cold or hot conditions due to their unique inherited genes.

The Russians believe that the plant existed in the Pleistocene Epoch, during the last Ice Age—and, in true *Ice Age* movie fashion, it is believed to have been buried there by a squirrel. Prehistoric rodents survived this era by digging burrows in the ice, leading to intricate tunnel systems. These burrows are believed to be the size of a soccer ball, and the animals create the perfect food-preservation ground by first adding hay and then a layer of animal fur. It is believed that the squirrel's contribution to sustainability makes the perfect cryobank (sperm bank) for plants.

What other magical discoveries await us in the future—and which amazing stories lay behind them?

The Italian Spider Dance

You'll instantly recognize the tune of a Tarantella dance, albeit you might not know the name of the song at first. What you also might not know is the rich history behind this Italian folk dance.

Before this was used as an upbeat tune at weddings and other festivals, the Tarantella had another use altogether. The dance was born in the small town of Taranto in the Puglia region. The locals called it the "dance of the spider."

It all dates back to the 15th–17th centuries in old Italy, where the prevalence of tarantulas was widespread. Folk then believed that a bite from this arachnid was toxic and led to an occurrence called tarantism. Many peasant women (*tarantata*) worked in the fields and subsequently got bitten by the *tarantola* (tarantula). Some of the symptoms associated with the bite included restlessness, fever, blurry vision, tremors, shakes, and fainting spells, to name a few.

Apparently, the only anti-venom available at the time was to place the victim in the middle of the town square and call the musicians. Then, with musical instruments being furiously played, the victim would dance until they were exhausted and the effects of the poison had been expelled via sweating from the dance—and with it, a cure was born!

The good news is that today, it's used as a dance of seduction where two pairs (two men and two women) perform a dance-off, where the ladies dance and play the tambourine all while trying to impress the men in the proud tri-colors of Italy. However, superstitious individuals will tell you that it's not advisable to dance the Tarantella solo or with a pair of the same gender—it's said to bring incredible bad luck.

The Most Crowded Island in the World

Just off the coast of Colombia, you'll find the most densely populated island on our planet. The tiny island of Santa Cruz del Islote is located in the archipelago of San Bernardo, and it's a far cry from what you'd probably expect. It's nothing more than a strip of land measuring 12,000 square meters, but it boasts a population of 1,247 inhabitants—making the island four times more populated than New York City's Manhattan Island in the United States.

Apparently, the island strip was discovered 150 years ago by a fisherman party seeking new waters to fish in. They stumbled on the island, fished, and decided to spend the night. The following morning, much to their delight, they discovered they had no mosquito bites on their bodies—an uncommon occurrence for the area—and made a decision on the spot to make the island their permanent home.

Apparently, there are over 155 houses on the island and even a school that only goes up to the 10th grade. The inhabitants are said to live a simplistic life with no available sewage system and a generator that only powers for five hours daily. Colombian naval ships supply their drinking water every three weeks, and the deceased are buried on islands nearby.

Furthermore, the island's residents work on resorts nearby and live off catching fish.

Another interesting fact about this colorful island village is that it formed the base camp of the third installment of the *Deep Blue Sea* movie franchise.

When Athletes Bite

Luis Suarez—Soccer

One can't help but wonder what goes on in the mind of an adult human being when they chomp on another—and when they are a sports celebrity, it makes us ponder away even more! One such athlete is Mr. Suarez, whose current total stands at three incidents.

In November 2010, while playing for club Ajax, soccer player Luis Suarez bit the shoulder of a fellow player Otman Bakkal during a match. He was allowed to continue the game, even though it happened right in front of the referee. Later, he was sanctioned with a seven-game ban and a hefty fine from his club.

It didn't end there, though. In 2013, Suarez, then playing for Liverpool, delivered another bite, this time to the arm of an unsuspecting victim. This referee also left him to complete the game. It seemed Luis didn't learn his lesson the first time and was slapped with a 10-match ban this time around.

A year later, during the 2014 FIFA World Cup, he chomped down on Italian soccer player Giorgio Chiellini and was also not punished on the spot after leaving teeth indentations on his opponent's shoulder. In all three instances in which he bit his opponents, he was allowed to continue playing in the matches, only to be punished later. Sometimes, fact is just stranger than fiction!

Anthony Watts—Rugby

As we continue our journey into biting athletes, this time, we go to the world of rugby. Our next story will have any male reading this book involuntarily cringe in pain. You see, apparently, rugby player Anthony Watts bit an opponent mid-match on his nether regions (of all places) back in 2002!

Watts and the opposing team member were involved in a scrap for the ball close to the try line. The next moment, the bitee was seen rolling around on the field in pain, signaling to the referee that he had been bitten on his member. The result? Watts got an eight-match ban, although he rubbished any such claims. Seems like a minor punishment compared to Suarez's incidents, doesn't it?

Mike Tyson—Boxing

It seems like contact sports tend to bring out the biter in athletes. The most notorious chomping incident of all has to be the boxing bout between bitter rivals Mike Tyson and Evander Holyfield. Taking a bite from Holyfield's ear on June 28, 1997, brought Tyson's career to an abrupt end, as he was slapped with a lifetime ban from the sport he loves so much.

Wrongful Witch Executions

In colonial Massachusetts between 1692 and 1693, a widespread paranoia reared its ugly head. As a result, 200 people were wrongfully convicted, and 20 were executed after being accused of dabbling in what was then termed as "Devil's Magic." It's one of history's saddest tales of injustice, as the colony later admitted that these trials and executions were a mistake. Yet, more than 300 years later, the Salem Witch Trials still fascinate people to this day!

During the 1300s to 1600s, witchcraft mania was a widespread fear-mongering where religious purists were of the opinion that the devil himself bestowed supernatural powers to certain individuals to do his bidding in harming them. All the commotion created a divide between the village's inhabitants, and many believed that the local reverend himself was one of Satan's followers.

In 1962, the reverend's daughter and niece both started having episodic fits where they would scream profanities, throw objects around in anger, and contort themselves into strange positions. Later, another girl displayed similar symptoms. All three incidents were blamed on three women:

1. Sarah Osborne, a poor, elderly woman

2. Sarah Good, a beggar

3. Tituba, the reverend's slave

All three women were brought to trial. The first two women maintained that they were innocent, but Tituba went on to admit guilt and added sordid details to her testimony. As a result, all three women were sentenced to jail. In addition, 17 other incidents took place, and the other "perpetrators" were also sent to jail.

In 1697, the judge, jury, and executioners admitted guilt and error in their judgment, albeit much too late. As a result, the General Court declared a day of soul-searching and fasting. In 1702, the Salem Witch Trials were officially declared as an unlawful act, and in 1711, those tried and executed had their good names restored and their families were paid a "consolation" of around $820.

Much later, in 1976, psychologist Linnda Caporael published a study in the journal *Science*. She made a concrete conclusion that the symptoms experienced by the victims could very well be attributed to a fungus called ergot. When the fungi are consumed, they yield similar results to those described in the story. In addition, Salem's balmy, damp climate provided a perfect breeding ground for the fungus, which was found to be present on staples such as rye during the time in question.

The First English-Speaking English King

Before the year 1066 (before the Norman conquest), most English kings spoke either a Saxon dialect or French rather than their native tongue. All were believed to have varying understanding of what was called Middle English at the time. None other than William the Conqueror established French as the official language during his reign.

By the turn of the 14th century, most of the royals and heir apparent could converse in and understand English and French as spoken by their subjects.

English was only made the official language in 1362 by the *Statute of Pleading* when all the nobles and the then-reigning kings could conduct business affairs in their home language. However, the first English king to adopt English as his first language was Henry IV, a.k.a Henry Bolingbroke (inaugurated in the 15th century). Later, his son, Henry V, also used it as the preferred language for personal communication.

So, why did Henry IV adopt English as his first language? French was initially viewed as the language of the upper class and the nobles, with English deemed the language of peasants. More and more, the French language lost appeal and control in France (because the peasants could speak French, too), and in 1450 it became easier to converse in English. Many modern royals and nobles are still fluent in French, but they only use it to converse with French-speaking people.

Other interesting English language facts:

- Norman-French is still spoken in the British-owned Channel Islands.

- It's believed that before English was adopted as the official language, most Norman kings preferred to swear in English rather than French (it seems even in those days, nothing got the message across more than an explosive f-bomb).

- New York City was briefly dubbed New Orange (after William the Conqueror) in 1673 when the Dutch captured the city.

Vietnam's Crazy House

There are many architectural marvels worldwide, and Vietnam's Hang Nga Guesthouse, or "crazy house," is no different. In between the Dalat's province of other French colonial villas, this complex structure definitely catches the eye. The piece of art is the brainchild of artist Dang Viet Nga, the daughter of former Vietnam General Secretary Truong Chinh.

After completing her Ph.D. in architecture in Moscow, she toured Vietnam with her son and fell in love with the green landscapes and rich history. She was tired of creating mundane, everyday structures that limited her creativity.

In February of 1990, she started drafting the plans for her crazy house. She let her imagination flow, and instead of producing blueprints, she painted. The paintings yielded different shapes and sizes of all-organic elements. She incorporated various wood, concrete, and steel components when construction started. What resulted was a product that could only come from something fable-like as depicted in the epic tale of *Hansel and Gretel*. Her idea was to bring the world closer to nature and preserve it for future generations—a project to this day she admits will never be completed.

The main house forms the epicenter of her work and is surrounded by four huge tree houses. Patrons and holidaymakers can traverse between the houses using a network of cement branches that double as bridges. Upon entering the treehouses, you are met with a series of ten guest rooms where her playful style is reflected. Each room is named after an animal or a plant and is awash with wooden seating areas and cavern-style beds promising a toasty night's rest to those seeking serenity in its confines.

Nga is in the process of dreaming up two new additions in the form of a Sky Garden and a Land Garden to add to the masterpiece. This will bring about many new nature-inspired crevices and crannies for visitors to explore and enjoy.

Who Invented Taekwondo?

The inventor of this martial art form, Choi Hong Hi, was born in 1918 in North Korea (then called the Myon Chun district). According to stories told, he was a frail child growing up. However, this sickly child became a protest leader at the tender age of 12 when he led a protest against the then-occupying Japanese. This saw his father take him to a tutor to study Chinese calligraphy. This tutor also took the fragile boy and trained him in the art of Korean foot fighting.

In 1937, he went to Japan, where he pursued studies in karate, math, and English. However, in 1942, he returned to North Korea and was drafted into the Japanese army against his will. He tried his best to escape to join the underground Korean Liberation Army, but he was caught and sentenced to prison after being labeled a traitor. Luckily, he was released in August 1945, mere days before his execution was set to take place.

By 1946, he co-formed the South Korean army and eventually became its general. In the process, Taekwondo was born, and he trained all and sundry under his command in the new martial art form. It was a combination of karate (Japanese) and taek kyon (Korean). Later, he became a mentor and hosted train-the-trainer sessions, passing this new form of defense on to other instructors to teach. In 1966, he established the International Taekwondo Federation and the sport became widespread in Asia, North America, and Western Europe. It even went so far as becoming the preferred combat method of several nations' armies.

This did not sit well with the South Korean army, and they became fearful that the martial art form would be used against them. As a result, they denied General Choi's request to teach Taekwondo in North Korea. Choi was irate at the fact that his art form and sport was being used as political propaganda and decided to go into voluntary exile by settling in Canada. To add insult to injury, South Korea created a rival association in Seoul called the World Tae Kwon Do Federation. It used Choi's term, but many rules and positions differed. General Choi passed away from a long battle with stomach cancer in Toronto on June 15, 2002.

Crazy Historical Facts About Coca-Cola

There is probably not one person in modern society who doesn't know at least what Coca-Cola—or Coke, for short—looks and tastes like. But did you know the following facts?

Yip, it contained cocaine at one point!

No, this is not a legend. In a 1996 article published by the *New York Times*, a spokesperson for the popular beverage brand confirmed as much. They said that in the late 19th century, when Coca-Cola was first created, it did contain actual elements from the coca plant. These days, it boasts a non-narcotic extract of the same plant. It's also important to remember that prior to 1914, drugs like cocaine weren't illegal or frowned upon. Interesting, right? Even today, many people claim an addiction to the drink.

The recipe is kept in a secret vault

Although the manufacturer will never let anyone see the actual 125-year-old recipe, you can definitely see the place it's being kept. The Vault of the Secret Formula is apparently located at the Coca-Cola Museum in Atlanta. Before this secure room, it was stored under lock and key in another secret vault at the SunTrust Bank, also in Atlanta. However, the beverage giant decided to move the recipe to a new location as part of its 125th celebration.

It was the first soda in space

Coke became the first soft drink in space when it was consumed by the astronauts on the Challenger space shuttle on July 12, 1985. Coca-Cola made use of the opportunity by testing the "Coca-Cola Space Can" and even installed the Coke "Space Dispenser" onboard the shuttle.

A church in Mexico uses Coke during sermons

Not only is Mexico the biggest consumer of Coca-Cola, but one church also uses it during their Sunday services. Dubbed the "Coca-Cola" church, it is said that St. John's Baptist Church deploys Coke as part of their religious culture in-house. Apparently, church-goers are encouraged to consume the sweet, fizzy beverage. Then, when they burp, all evil is purged from body and soul.

The Coca-Cola font is patented

Apart from hidden images on promotional cans, even Coke's signature typography is patented! You won't ever witness any other logo or product with the "Spencerian Script." Coca-Cola registered a trademark in 1893 with the US Patent Office.

A Quick Pause...

If this book has helped you in any way, we'd appreciate it if you left us a review on Amazon. Reviews are the lifeblood of our business. We read every single one and incorporate your feedback into our future book projects.

To leave an Amazon review please visit https://www.amazon.com/ryp.

Can Stevie Wonder See?

Stevie Wonder has to be one of the most iconic music stars of the 20th century. But there have been a few times where it's been speculated that he is, in fact, not blind and has been faking it all along!

One instance was back in 2014, when Wonder performed a tribute to The Beatles on stage by singing his rendition of "Hey Jude." The mic came loose from the stand, and Stevie was caught on film catching it before it tumbled to the floor. Two years later, in 2016, Wonder was an award presenter at the Grammys and apparently opened the winning envelope after "looking down at it."

New life was breathed into the rumors when conspiracy theorists jumped to conclusions when the singer was shown on a TMZ video stating that he "landed" and "flown a plane" and that he will be "revealing the truth." NBA legend Shaquille O'Neal also recounted a story of when he met Wonder in a chance encounter in a building elevator and was immediately greeted by the singer.

Other famous celebrities are also siding with the non-blind tribe with their own theories, such as his lifelong friend Lionel Richie also believing that he is bluffing. He told the story of how he visited his friend at his house, and Wonder wanted him to listen to a song. Not only did Stevie put the tape in the cassette slot of the car radio, but he also drove the car and parked it perfectly! Perhaps it's because Stevie loves to sit courtside during basketball games and has the uncanny ability to use cameras quite effectively?

The Most Dangerous Tennis Court in the World

The year is 2005. Two of the tennis world's most notable male players (Roger Federer and Andre Agassi) agree to play on what is dubbed as the world's deadliest… tennis court! Why? The director of the Dubai Tennis Championship needed a Hail Mary to revive a dying sport in the county.

The players engaged in a round of this ball-and-racket sport on a converted helipad that offered no safety in terms of boundaries or fencing of any sort. Once both players agreed, the director enlisted the services of the five-star Burj Al-Arab luxury hotel's designated chopper landing spot, which is 212 m (695 ft) from the ground. The match took place on the 22nd of February, much to the fans and players' delight. It took Roger a mere 52 minutes to defeat veteran Agassi 6–3, 6–1.

The conversion totaled a whopping $25,000, but that day history was made when Federer suggested that a helicopter be used to film a 360-degree aerial view of the match instead of still shots from the hotel only. Apparently, this added to the appeal of the event. Later that year, Federer won the Dubai Championship—must have been all that death-defying practice so high up in the air.

London Actress Falls for an Alien

Well, the jury isn't out as yet, but apparently, "the truth is still out there"—or is it? London actress Abbie Bela was tired of the sea of fishes on Earth, so she decided to look out-of-species for love, instead.

She is making outlandish claims that she was first swept up by a charming alien in a proverbial white UFO and then ended up falling in love. The pandemic and the earthly dating world didn't impress her, so she started putting it out there that she wanted to be abducted. Shortly after that, she began having dreams of what she describes as a "white light." Then, she apparently received another message that told her to "wait in the usual spot." She claims to have never heard the voice before but seemed to understand precisely what it meant.

The following evening, she sat waiting by her open window and subsequently fell asleep. Then, around 12:15 a.m., she was apparently woken by a flying saucer, and the next thing she knew, she found herself inside the UFO, surrounded by five aliens.

She recounts that she couldn't see their true form but could make out their slender, tall silhouettes with a green-hued skin tone and large black eyes with humanistic features. They are even said to have eyebrows like Homo sapiens! She was told that she wasn't ready yet to see them in their intended forms.

Abbie said she didn't feel frightened for even a second—quite the opposite, as it was love at first sight for her when she "connected" with one of the otherworldly beings. She apparently felt the chemistry between them, and the alien reciprocated.

Sadly, he told her that a love match between humans and aliens was against the rules, but he would break the rules for her if she was willing to make the sacrifice of going back to (wherever) with them. Abbie, however, wasn't prepared to leave planet Earth just yet, and much less on the spot—she had concerns about whether she would be able to return afterward. So, after denying their request, she found herself back at home a short 20 minutes later and pondering the differences between alien men and earthmen.

She plans on being a champion of interspecies dating in the near future. But, for now, she keeps hoping that her interstellar lover will return and risk possible capture by the CIA. She even has an overnight bag packed if he were to risk it all again for a night of romance—and perhaps, just perhaps, she won't return this time!

Having Hair on Your Teeth

Among pubescent teenagers, the first discovery of hair in places you've never had before is almost like a rite of passage. But more than a decade after it was reported, scientists—and the world, for that matter—are still scratching their heads at the curious case of one Italian woman growing hair in her teeth, of all places!

She traveled to the University of Campania Luigi Vantelli in search of answers. There, she was diagnosed with a rare condition called *gingival hirsutism*. Their published article detailed that the woman first sought treatment in 2009 when hairs resembling eyelashes kept growing from her upper gums behind her two front teeth.

Physicians at the time diagnosed her with polycystic ovary syndrome (PCOS). This medical occurrence means that the patient suffers from a sexual hormone imbalance that results in excessive hair growth. She was prescribed birth control pills and later elected to have oral surgery to remove the hair from her teeth.

At first, it seemed that the first bout of treatment worked, but in 2015 the hair was back in full force. Not only were the hairs growing from behind her gums, but they were now manifesting on her chin and neck regions, too. So, she went back to the doctor for a second time, and sans the surgery, the same course of treatment was to be followed, only this time they told her to return in a year for another assessment. Let's just say that by the third time she went back, even more hair had grown in her mouth.

Doctors decided to perform a biopsy from a section of her gums and found that unusually thick hair shafts were pushing through the gum tissue. One theory that emerged is that when we are embryos, the oral mucosal tissue is closely related to that of our skin, where hair grows. So having them in your mouth is not unheard of, but producing oral hair is just plain weird!

The Italian woman is only one of six recorded cases of gingival hirsutism in history. Out of these patients, she is the only female, and all other cases date back to the 60s. So, with no cure in sight, the lady has to have hair on her teeth for the foreseeable future.

Did Sandy Die in *Grease*?

The 1978 movie *Grease* boasts an impressive star-studded cast, upbeat musical numbers, and a storyline teenage dreams are made of. But, of course, in true Hollywood style, no notable movie will escape fan-made conspiracy theories. Far away from the heartwarming tale of high-school romance is a much darker side, hidden behind the fanfare.

Remember the scene where Danny and Sandy first meet during school holidays on the beach? Well, some fans are hypothesizing that Sandy actually died by drowning on the beach, and Danny tried to save her. To add to the crazy, these fans attest that certain lyrics of the song "Summer Nights" and the opening and closing scenes prove the theory.

So, the conspiracy theorists are saying that she died in the opening sequence and it's suggested that she is now in heaven because they drive off in Danny's car to the skies at the end.

Two lines of the lyrics, in particular, are adding to the dark theory: "I saved her life, she nearly drowned," and "I've got chills; they're multiplying." Lastly, the line "down in the sand" seems to imply the fantasy of a dying girl on the beach as people helplessly try to revive her. So, to summarize, the whole movie suggests that while Sandy is fighting for her life, she is dreaming the whole musical and dies at the end en route to heaven and the Big Man upstairs.

Of course, die-hard *Grease* fans will disagree with the suggested dark fantasy, but to this day, no one really knows what the movie's end really implies. In the last end-of-year sequence, it seems that everyone is wide awake after Danny and the T-Birds dreamed about how the car will add to their sex appeal, and another, Frenchy had a fearful dream about what would happen if her attempts at becoming a beautician failed. However, everyone seems to be lucid and living in the now, so the fact that the movie ends with an unrealistic ending doesn't make sense at this point.

Is there any truth to the claims? Best you make up your own mind.

The World's Largest Open-Air Museum

Located just outside of Bangkok is the world's largest open-air museum. And if you're wondering why it boasts this accolade from the *Ripley's Believe It or Not!* files, it's because it's the size of 227 football fields all put together!

This structure occupies no less than 300 acres and its grounds, called Muang Boran, is in the shape of Thailand, as can be seen on the world map. This magnificent site plays host to no less than 116 life-size replicas of Asia's most significant monuments.

The name Muang Boran (translated as Ancient City) was created by a millionaire businessman by the name of Lek Viriyaphan, who also contributed to the funding of the Erawan Museum, also located in Bangkok.

When he bought the piece of land in the Samut Prakan area in 1963, he originally wanted to build a golf course surrounded by famous Thai moments as part of the decorations and design. Along the way, he got so inspired, he ended up building a historic tourist attraction instead of a signature 18-hole golf course.

Viriyaphan enlisted the help of the Bangkok National Museum, local architecture students, and even muralists to make his dream come alive. The grounds were divided into four different regions, meaning guests would be in the appropriate spot where they would find the replicas geographically, if they were to travel to the regions in question.

It's great that you can view all of Thailand's most impressive monuments in one place—however, if you're pressed for time, it's advisable to hire a bike or a golf cart on your tour, as the Muang Boran is simply too vast to explore in only one day.

Jobless South African Man Builds a Helicopter

In 2015, Vusimuzi Mbatha was a jobless man from an informal settlement in South Africa's Eastern Cape province. He was a big dreamer who decided to turn that dream into reality. His dream? He wanted to pilot a helicopter!

He saw a helicopter up close for the first time earlier that year, after seeing it fly low near the settlement where he lived at the time. Later, he said the project was an easy feat for him, all thanks to the vision in his mind.

Slowly but surely, Mbatha managed to scrape the parts together, buying the items he required one by one. The materials he used were all recycled, obtained from a scrapyard. His giant creation rests on top of his house and visitors travel from far and wide to marvel at its unbelievable glory.

The whole contraption sits on the four wheels of a trolley, with a cockpit created from soft drink crates. Nestled inside the cockpit is a TV set, a two-way radio, and lastly, an alarm clock. Vusimuzi plans on using the clock to record his estimated flight time when the time comes. But wait, there's more: the chopper even has a working engine. Mbatha built the engine using a gas-powered motorbike battery, which is used to propel and power the motor. The actual rotor hub is encased in a soft drink crate, and the steering mechanism is rounded off with an old Playstation control. P.S. It even has an accelerator and a clutch.

Vusimuzi's tale is really an inspiring one. He came to the North West province (where he now lives) from his hometown 16 years ago in the hopes of securing employment at one of the mines. He absolutely adores science, but sadly he had to drop out of school in the seventh grade due to financial constraints and, with that, his dreams faded. Despite his creation enjoying much media attention, Mbatha remains unemployed to this day!

The moral of the story? You can if you want to!

Oak Island's Money Pit

HISTORY's *Curse of Oak Island* has been leaving fans of the show on the edge of their seats since 2014. It follows the adventures of brothers Rick and Marty Laguna in their pursuit of finding the so-called Money Pit, said to be located on a tiny island off the Nova Scotian coast. Legend goes that a great treasure is hidden there, dating back over 200 years. Even ex-President Teddy Roosevelt has been among those hoping to uncover the secret, but so far in vain. There has been much speculation about what exactly has been buried here, and the theories range from pirate treasure to the Ark of the Covenant, straight down to the Holy Grail.

In the television series, the two brothers can be seen digging up ancient sites, and history dictates that some valuable artifacts and priceless relics have been uncovered there in the past. But what exactly is the Money Pit? This is believed to be a shaft of around 100 m (3.28 ft) deep. The first discovery was made in 1795 by a group of teenagers who noticed a curious indentation in the ground, and they started digging. They stumbled across a man-made shaft with a series of wooden platforms every 3 m (10 ft).

In the 60s, on one treasure mission, the shaft was hidden away due to a range of holes that were dug and subsequently collapsed. Today, the two Laguna bros dig in and around the holes they believe to be in close proximity to the original shaft. Unfortunately, it appears that the holes surrounding the shaft are said to be boobytrapped as the brothers' efforts are brought to a grinding halt around every corner. As soon as they reach a certain depth, the hole fills back up with water, stymieing them back to square one.

But why all the fuss? This is due to the origin of the story itself being a mystery. Many believe that it's merely a legend, while others go as far as to believe that the Money Pit is the location of the Knights Templar treasure. Keep in mind that previous treasure seekers have also all put their own spin on the tale— probably in a bid to throw everyone else off the scent.

One tale in particular states that the site is cursed and the treasure will only be found or a solution will manifest after seven men have died. So far, the tally is six in total. Will the Laguna brothers escape the curse and make the discovery of a lifetime? Only time will tell!

Nikumaroro Island and Amelia Earhart

One of the most noteworthy theories about the disappearance of aviatrix Amelia Earhart and her navigator Fred Noonan in 1937 is that they crashed close to Garner island (now called Nikumaroro). The last they were heard from was when they radioed that they were running out of gas, and then there was only silence. One theory suggests that they were taken by the Japanese as prisoners because WWII started in the same year, and a picture was later found of two European-looking individuals on a dock, said to be Noonan and Earhart. At the time the picture was taken (rumored to be in the 30s), the island was under the control of Japanese Marshals. Others believe that they simply crashed into the ocean.

So, why is Nikumaroro island being brought into question? One theory suggests that they did, in fact, survive the crash and lived on the island until their death. This is due to an empty jar of Earhart's freckle cream (she is said to have hated her freckles) being found on the island, as well as a piece of acrylic fragment believed to be part of her missing Lockheed Electra 10e, in addition to some unidentified bones.

The bones were found on the island in 1940, though they remain unidentified. While they were first believed to be that of a man and not a woman, more recent evidence suggests that the person who initially examined the remains made a mistake. There is no further evidence to suggest the bones aren't hers, so it is currently assumed that, unless proven otherwise, the remains are Earhart.

The latest story that came to light in May 2021 was that a gent named Mike Ashmore was using Apple Maps to explore Nikumaroro online and came across an anomaly that resembled plane wreckage in a shallow watery grave. Stay tuned for further developments on the story.

We are still yet to discover what happened on the fateful day of July 2, 1937, when Amelia Earhart disappeared, and until then, the conspiracy theories will continue to surface. However, explorers definitely agree on one thing: the clues and evidence of what happened to Amelia and Fred are out there, waiting to be found.

That Time We Got Alien Messages and Music

"Outer-spacey music"

In the year 1969, a group of Apollo 10 astronauts were mid-lunar orbiting around the moon when they heard an eerie sound, described as a strange, whistling sound. At first, they weren't sure if they needed to say anything to the rest of the world, as they thought no one would believe them anyway!

The Apollo 10 mission paved the way for the big moon landing of Neil Armstrong and the rest of his Apollo 11 crew some two months later. With them, it appears the conspiracy of hearing "outer-spacey" music died. It turns out (apparently) that there is a perfectly non-alien explanation for the weird whistling sound. It became public knowledge in the 70s that the tune is a result of VHF radio interference from the two vehicles that Apollo 10 used to orbit the moon—two were in a lunar module and one was in a command module, approximately 10 miles above the surface.

In 2012, NASA added the audio transcripts and actual audio files online where they can be read and listened to.

Alien signals

Astronomer Jerry Ehman was on duty in August of 1977. His job? He was tasked to look at computer readouts from the Big

Ear telescope, analyzing them to see if alien life was trying to send messages to Earth. That night, he actually found an anomaly.

One evening, the telescope was calibrated to focus on the star *Chi Saggritti* as part of the message-finding mission. Being a volunteer at the time, Ehman was part of the SETI (extraterrestrial intelligence) program. While scanning a printout, he noticed a rare sequence of numbers: 6EQUJ5. Even many years later, this string of numerics is considered the strongest indication of life on other planets trying to communicate with us.

Jerry called the phenomena the "Wow! signal." Big Ear picked up the odd signal on a burst of narrowband radio waves at 1,420 megahertz. Now, in most cases, narrowband frequencies are believed to be man-made, and wideband frequencies are normally caused by stars and galaxies.

In the years after the signal was received, many people hypothesized what exactly could be the cause of the Wow! signal. In 2016, Antonio Paris, another astronomer, came up with an interesting explanation. He said that two comets called 335P/Gibbs and 266P/Christensen (only discovered after the Wow! signal) would've been observed during that same night. Science dictates that comets release bursts of hydrogen, and the 1,420 megahertz frequency is one of the primary instances where the hydrogen atoms absorb and emit energy—thus explaining the reading that Ehman received.

The jury is still out on both of these instances, adding to the mystery and excitement of whether we are alone in the universe... or not.

Armando—The World's Most Expensive Pigeon

In 2019, a Belgian-bred pigeon sold for a staggering 10,52,22,255.73 Indian Rupees ($1,410,320 USD), making this bird the most expensive living pigeon on the planet. Armando, dubbed the Lewis Hamilton of the bird-racing world, is the country's fastest racer in history.

Racing pigeons are different from wild pigeons. They are home-reared and highly trained. Pigeon racing works on the premise of the birds being released and then timing their movement to find the bird that returns home the quickest, which is then crowned the winner of the race. The formula used to determine the winner is based on the allotted time the pigeon took to get home and its rate of movement compared to its competitors. There is a specific species of pigeon used for these races called the Racing Homer (fitting, don't you think?). It is said that these birds can race in distances spanning anything from 100 km (62 mi) to 1,000 km (620 mi).

The Most "Kissed" Girl in the World

The "*L'Inconnue de la Seine*," or the Unknown Woman of the Seine, is a sad tale of a girl from 19th-century Paris, France, who tragically drowned in the Seine river. It's presumed that she was a teenager at the time. In attempting to identify Jane Doe, the authorities who pulled her from the river decided to put her corpse on display in a mortuary.

The coroner, mesmerized by the apparent peaceful look on the girl's face, created a death mask (plaster cast) of her facial expression. Later on, her face served as the model used in dummy CPR training.

The inspiration came in the late 50s–60s when CPR and mouth-mouth resuscitation was invented. One Arthur Gordon from the American Heart Association noticed that the medical students who performed these actions during their practical assessment were injuring one another. So, together with fellow Dr. Bjorn Lind, he approached toy manufacturer Åsmund Laerdal to create a life-like doll that the students could use for training purposes. Laerdal was eager to produce a mannequin for them. Having seen a replica of the Unknown Woman of the Seine, he used this as a prototype for Gordon and Lind's doll. It is said that her serene features are not intimidating, and subsequently, what we now know as "Annie," or "*Rescuci Anne*," was born.

The Laerdal company still makes the CPR dolls to this day. To date, it is estimated that 300 million people worldwide received their CPR certifications using a replica of Rescuci Anne, dubbing her the most "kissed" girl in the world. Stories like this really can't be made up!

Houdini's Last Act

The most celebrated magician-slash-escape-artist of the 20th century has to be none other than Erik Weisz, better known by his famous stage name, Harry Houdini. This man seemed to have cheated death more times than any other person operating in the same hemisphere.

So much so, even, that the manner in which Houdini left this earth is a highly debatable topic, centuries later. The escape artist was known to be an individual with high pain tolerance who simply continued working when ill or injured after his stunts. One example thereof is when (mere weeks before his passing), he battled a fractured ankle but continued performing his renowned Chinese Water Cell Torture act. Instead of seeking medical attention, he continued on his tour.

One fateful night, he was nursing his ankle in his Montreal dressing room, surrounded by three students. One of them (Joselyn Gordon Whitehead) asked Houdini about his claims that he could withstand any blow to his stomach. To this day, it's not known if Harry bragged about it, but he replied that it was true.

When Whitehead received the positive response from Houdini, he asked if he could put the man's claims to the test.

Again, the escape artist confirmed, but the legend goes that Houdini wasn't quite ready for the onslaught that followed.

It's said that Whitehead immediately jumped up from his seat and started pounding Harry in the stomach. He did so four or five times consecutively before Houdini asked him to stop. Harry claimed to be fine afterward, but by the following day, he ran a fever of 104 degrees and complained of excruciating stomach pains.

He continued to perform against the wishes of the advising physician, and that evening, he was unable to complete his act and rushed to the hospital. Doctors found that his appendix had ruptured and proceeded to remove it. Sadly, it was too late, and Houdini is said to have died from peritonitis post-surgery a week later on Halloween.

Debatable circumstances aside, the fact that this larger-than-life persona passed away from something as mundane as peritonitis is still a mystery to his admirers. First off, an autopsy was never performed to substantiate the exact cause of death. Secondly, it was never established if the blows to the stomach caused the appendix to rupture or if it was completely unrelated. Others said he passed away after being poisoned by spiritualists (mediums) because he called them out on their fake acts of talking to the dead.

It seems this is another mystery that we'll never have the true answer to regarding what caused the demise of the man known as Harry Houdini.

Pop Goes the Popsicle

The tale of how the Popsicle came to be is a curious one that sounds like it could've been made up. For one, it was a purely incidental creation by an 11-year-old lad called Frank Epperson and was born on his front porch.

One day in 1905, the boy made himself a beverage by mixing soda powder and water in a glass and left a wooden stirrer inside the glass. In true child fashion, he forgot about his soft drink and left it outside overnight.

That night, the temperature outside dropped to below freezing. The next morning, when he remembered his drink, Frank found the soda mixture was completely frozen and stuck to the wooden stick. He had, overnight, created the planet's first Popsicle. He called it the Epsicle and made more to sell to the other kids in his hometown.

As Frank grew older, he forgot about his magical invention and became a lemonade salesman. Later, he progressed from sales and started his career as a realtor with the Realty Syndicate Company in California. The year 1922 saw him bring his Epsicle back to life by creating the iced lolly and taking it to some local firemen at their year-end ball. Needless to say, they were just as popular that day as when he was a child. The next year, Frank filed a patent, which he received in 1924. The patent was issued for "a handled, frozen confection or ice lollipop." The name "Popsicle" came from his children because their dad had invented the frozen treat.

After receiving the patent, he sold his popsicles at Neptune Beach's amusement park and boasted seven different flavors. Sadly, hard times hit, and he was forced to sell his prized patent in 1925 to the Joe Lowe Company in New York. Joe Lowe took the popsicle to the next level. In the first rotation, the sticks were first made from birch wood and sold for a nickel. Eventually, it was modified to have two sticks so that two kids could share.

In 1965, Consolidated Foods Corporation bought the brand, and in 1986, the US branch of Popsicle Industries merged with the Gold Bond Ice Cream Company in Green Bay, Wisconsin. Since 1989, Popsicle has been part of the Unilever brand in the US with its very own division.

Today, it's believed that Epperson's creation also served as inspiration for other treats—the Dreamsicle, Creamsicle, and the Fudgsicle. More than 30 different flavors are available at most supermarket chains in and around the United States.

Monster in the Amazon

With the Amazon rainforest being a vast place of beauty, it should come as no surprise that there are certain scary tales and legends about "monsters," too. Some claim to have seen them, and others have called hogwash on those claims. No matter if it's true or not, the tale of the mapinguary is said to be that of a scary and hairy, large sloth-like monster.

There are many Indian tribes in the forest, and even though some of them have never had contact with one another, almost every tribe knows exactly what you are talking about when you mention the word "mapinguary." The name means "the fetid beast" or "the roaring animal."

The stories have been so rife and constant that many an expedition have occurred to search for the elusive, giant beast. Unfortunately, none of the excursions so far has successfully achieved a sighting, but one adventurer says that he can explain the creature and its origins.

David Oren, a former research director at the Goeldi Institute in Belém, believes the Indian tribes are referring to a now-extinct creature, the ground sloth widespread in the Amazon thousands of years ago. It is known that the species previously thought to be extinct has been found many years after it was believed to be gone. However, it is unconfirmed whether the mapinguary has survived in modern times.

During his studies, Oren is said to have talked to over a hundred people who have all claimed to have encountered the roaring animal or have at least seen it from afar. Of course, different pictures are painted about what the monster looks like, but they all seem to agree that the animal is at least seven feet tall, with a lot of tangled hair covering a hard outer structure (said to be bulletproof). But the most remarkable description of all is that everyone agrees that this thing stinks—big time!

Some tribespeople claim to have tried killing it in the past and assert it could only be killed by delivering a fatal shot to the head. However, just like a skunk, the beast seems to use this foul odor to deter hunters. Apparently, the stench is so potent, hunters faint or get dizzy on the spot.

True or not, it's clear that the fascination with the mapinguary will be around for quite some time. However, we should also take into account that the Amazon forest is a large area—just because we don't have conclusive proof that the mapinguary exists, it doesn't mean it's not out there, freely roaming the woods.

Bell Did NOT Invent the Telephone

Okay, so we were all taught in school about Alexander Graham Bell, credited as the inventor of the telephone—or is he? Some say Antonio Santi Giuseppe Meucci was the actual inventor of the device we know today, but is that true?

Meucci, an Italian immigrant, has many proud inventions under his belt, and one such device provided a method for communicating sound waves across a distance—meaning it was basically a telephone. Legend dictates that Antonio invented the world's first phone some 150 years before Bell did.

Taking a trip back to the 1800s, a terrific time for inventions in Italy, we find Meucci just finishing his degree and working at the famous Teatro Della Pergola Operahouse, where he designed and built stages. Meucci crafted a device that was used between the control room and the stage in 1834. The invention was a set of acoustic pipes that used sound waves to communicate.

Even though Meucci battled to raise the required funds to support his inventions, he never gave up on his dream. On December 12, 1871, together with three other individuals, he established the *Telettrofono* Company. This company was responsible for the commercialization of Meucci's sound telegraph.

In 1872, Meucci filed paperwork for the first patent of the telephone. Unfortunately, he omitted to mention that the vocal sounds were transmitted via electromagnetism, and the bill expired in 1875. Three years later, in 1878, Bell responded by filing all the correct documentation, and this saw him being awarded the patent for the device we used today. The result? All the glory going to Bell and Meucci being overlooked in history with no credit to him for inventing the telephone. Let's be honest—he does deserve some credit for his ingenuity, don't you think?

The Missing 10 Babies, or is it Eight?

There have been numerous miraculous instances where mothers have given birth to multiple babies at a time, but ten is a lot! In June 2021, a picture of a heavily pregnant woman from South Africa was doing the rounds on social media. She claimed to have later given birth to no fewer than ten babies.

It wouldn't be the first time Gosiame Sithole had been blessed with many babies. She has a set of older twins with her partner, too. On June 8, 2021, it was reported to the world that Sithole gave birth to ten babies. Apparently, her partner Mr. Teboho Tsotetsi received the news via a text message, but due to COVID restrictions, he wasn't allowed near the hospital.

News traveled fast, and soon other news outlets like the BBC published the story. The curious part is that up until that point, no one had confirmed the news with the hospital where the births allegedly took place, and no one had even seen the ten babies yet.

The babies, dubbed the "Thembisa 10" (based on their hometown of birth), received many donations worldwide, including from the Interdependent Online (IOL) chairman, who contributed $63,176,74 (1,000,000 Rand). After the story was published, the rumors started to fly as the initial news outlet to report the story, the Pretoria News, refused to disclose the hospital where the babies were supposedly born. Other hospitals in the province also came out to deny any such incidents in the process.

Ten days after the supposed birth of the babies, IOL started making accusations against the Steve Biko Academic Hospital, where the babies were rumored to be born. Strangely enough, Gosiame was later reported as missing, and the donations were stopped on request. Then, Sithole turned around and accused a close friend, who allegedly contacted the Pretoria News, of wanting to benefit from the story financially.

Later, Sithole was tracked down by social workers and sent for tests. Since then, it was reported that the earlier leaked image was of the mother carrying eight babies, not ten. It was later discovered that no hospital in the Gauteng province had a record of such a large number of babies being born from the same mother, and the tests indicated that the 37-year-old mother was not pregnant recently.

Sithole is apparently being held under observation of the mental act of South Africa and is receiving the necessary support. Even though the Pretoria News stands by its reporting, no reasons were provided by Sithole's family spokesperson as to the need to fabricate such an outlandish feel-good piece.

Moberly and Jourdain—The Chrononauts

The year is 1901. On the 10th of August, two English lasses, Charlotte Anne Moberly and Eleanor Jourdain embarked on what would be the adventure of a lifetime to France. During their holiday, they decided to take a day tour to the Palace of Versailles.

Mid-tour, they visited a little château called *Petit Trianon*. It's located on the palace grounds and was a gift from King Louis XVI to his teenage Queen Marie Antoinette. He perfectly understood that she was young and needed a place away from the public eye, where the then 19-year-old could just be herself.

Moberly and Jourdain claim to have seen some strange events take place on their tour at the château. Bored with their guide, they decided to stroll around the gardens and got way more than they bargained for. The little manor house they wanted to explore was located in Grand Trianon park, and they found the entrance to the park to be closed.

They consulted their guidebook to find an alternative entrance but got miserably lost. Instead of following the *Allée des Deux Trianons* map, they mistakenly entered a small alley and completely missed the château.

They are said to have seen individuals donning clothing not from the current era, heard strange voices talking, and even saw structures and buildings that weren't present in 1901. They even went as far as saying they saw Marie Antoinette in person and that she was busily drawing in her sketchbook while sitting on the lawn in front of the manor house. Apart from all the visuals, the women also recount being overwhelmed by feelings of sadness and oppression.

Their explanation for the mysterious events is that they entered a time slip and became chrononauts (time travelers), and were retrospectively taken back in time over 100 years prior before being pulled back to the present by their tour guide.

No one is really sure if they did travel back in time. But some explanations assert they might've experienced what is called a joint delusion or a *folie a deux,* and others say what they saw was misconstrued. Just when it seemed that no one believed them, they jointly penned a book in 1911 called *An Adventure*, under the *noms de plume* Elizabeth Morison and Frances Lamont. You can still read the book today, republished under the name *The Ghosts of Trianon*. Their book tells the story of two chrononauts who were briefly transported back to pre-revolutionary France and all the characters they encountered. The question is, were they on to something or not?

Thames' River Swines

In a time when the Thames river is clogged with many pollutants and often flooded, it's hard to believe that there was a time Londoners could drink from the water, because it was so clean. But in the 16th century, wild boars were abundant along the Thames River and available for all to hunt.

Sounds made up, but before trashy B-rated movies made rounds on the circuits, the folk living in 1850 genuinely had a fear of aggressive pigs residing in London's sewers, especially those living in the system close to the River Thames. Many believed that hordes of foul-smelling wild hogs would come out and run amok in the city.

But where does the story come from in the first place? Well, according to a local folktale, a worker at the Smithfield market lost their prize sow in what is now known as The River Fleet Ditch. Further, if the legend is to be believed, this prized animal was said to be pregnant when she went missing and sought refuge in the sewer system. One story, in particular, suggests that the sow escaped a butcher's knife. Naturally, this resulted in fear-mongering stories manifesting that she was rearing her young in the sewer system from the filth and stench.

This discouraged many adventurers said to have participated in the novel concept of sewer spelunking, where one digs for treasure and lost items through layers of stinking muck. It's believed that the wild hogs lost their sense of domesticity and became rogue and aggressive, meaning they posed a threat to anyone entering their territory and "stealing their gems." Whether this is fact or myth, one thing is for sure: it gives new meaning to the phrase "casting pearls before swine."

Mummy in My Tummy

In modern society, we view things much differently than those who came before us. One thing in particular that causes this disconnect is death. For one, today, it's all about booking a service, selecting a coffin, and getting the affair handled as quickly as possible. In ancient eras, they took their time in performing funeral rituals and also spent time in mourning. One of the most fascinating characters of death has to be the mummies and the stories some of them have to tell.

In 1955, expectant mother Zahra Aboutalib excitedly went to the hospital to give birth to her long-awaited bundle of joy. She was in labor for an extensive amount of time but had not given birth, so her concerned physician ordered delivery by cesarean section. While doctors prepared the ER, she ran from the hospital. Sadly, as she did, the baby succumbed in her womb—but again, she didn't want to have the dead fetus removed.

Many years later, she started to experience knee-numbing pains in her stomach and went to the doctor. The physician ordered an X-ray and stumbled across what they believed to be a tumor. However, before doing anything rash, the doctor decided to perform more tests—and he found that it wasn't a growth, but the remains of her unborn child that was now calcified some 46 years later.

This rare condition is also called lithopedion, and it's said there are only 300 recorded cases so far. The process of lithopedion starts when a woman's body cannot rid the dead fetus from its confines. The body then goes into defense mode by protecting itself from possible infection due to the decomposition of dead tissue. The body's answer to this is to create layers of calcified elements around the dead baby, rendering the fetus a mummy, which is then called a stone baby.

Avril Lavigne 2.0?

Everyone's favorite "Girlfriend" and singer of other hit songs such as "Sk8ter Boi" has been the subject of conspiracy for many years. This is because the artist is said to have an uncanny ability to remain looking young throughout her career.

In 2021, she was part of the guestlist at that year's VMA award ceremony, and she looked every part the pop-punk princess we've come to know and love. Before the show started, she arrived on the red carpet in a blingy two-piece crafted from tartan. Twitter went berserk and said that it's not her but, in fact, her doppelganger/clone known to the internet trolls as Melissa.

Now, this isn't the first time that the story of an Avril lookalike has done the rounds. The first rumors started flying in 2005 when a fan page of the singer said that she had been making use of a body double since she became famous. Some Brazilian fans even said that the real Lavigne died and that the record label replaced her with Melissa to keep Avril's memory alive and the cash rolling in.

The fans are even claiming that there is proof that the faux Avril does exist, and they are pointing to specific instances during interviews where the fake is said to have messed up the interview, where the real singer would've aced it. Another factor that has fueled the crazy rumors is that the real Avril likes to wear trousers and Melissa seems to prefer dresses. Lastly, there are also rumors that in Lavigne's/Melissa's video of the hit song "Slipped Away," the singer has the word "Melissa" written on her hand as she belts out the lyrics, "The day you slipped away was the day I found it won't be the same."

Is this story true, or has Avril discovered the elusive Fountain of Youth elixir?

The Simpsons Accurately Predicted the Future

At the time of writing this book, everybody's favorite cartoon family was in its 33rd season, with one more in the works. The hit TV show *The Simpsons* has been gracing our television sets since December 17, 1989. But what few people know is that there have been numerous times (17 to date) where the show's creators accurately predicted future events, long before they eventually took place in real life. Some episodes include:

Lady Gaga's halftime show—May 20, 2012

In this episode, Lady Gaga is shown suspended high above the ground, singing at a live concert. Fast forward to the Superbowl LI halftime show on February 5, 2017, where the real Gaga did exactly that in an outfit that closely matched the one on the TV show.

Donald Trump's presidency—March 19, 2000

Sixteen years before Donald Trump was elected president, *The Simpsons* predicted it in an episode titled "Bart to the Future." It showed Lisa becoming the next Commander-in-Chief after the fictional Trump apparently killed the economy.

USA's Olympic gold medal for curling—February 14, 2010

In the episode "Boy Meets Curl," Marge and Homer are sent to the Winter Olympics and bag a gold medal in the curling event. In 2018, this prediction came true when the US Male Curling Team won the most unlikely of gold medals in the history of the sport at the Winter Olympic Games.

Smartwatches—sometime in 1995

It seems Apple was the second institution to invent smartwatches because *The Simpsons* beat them to it in 1995. In an episode of the show, the family is caught in the future, with one scene in particular where Lisa's husband is seen talking into a watch on his arm. Apple did not launch the first smartwatch until 2013.

Side note: Are the producers hinting at the fact that a person called Lisa will become the first female US President? It seems a bit funny that everything predicted so far is mainly centered around her in particular. What are your thoughts?

Disney acquires Fox—November 8, 1998

In an episode in 1998, there is a brief scene where the creators are teasing that Disney will acquire Fox, which would then become a division of Walt Disney Co. Well, in 2019, this came true when Disney completed their acquisition of Fox and all its assets.

What will *The Simpsons* correctly predict in the upcoming seasons—for those who pay attention?

Lesser Known Facts About the Mona Lisa

This timeless artwork from creator Leonardo da Vinci has to be one of the most recognizable portraits ever painted. If Mona Lisa were able to talk, she'd have many exciting stories to tell.

Her eyebrows (or lack thereof) is a bone of contention

When the portrait is viewed today, it seems as though the subject lacks eyebrows. Some scholars believe that the absence of facial hair implies that she was an upper-class lady of her time, and not having eyebrows was in fashion then. Other enthusiasts think the omission of the eyebrows is indicative that da Vinci never completed the portrait. Well, in 2007, all of the speculations were put to rest. Ultra HD scans of the painting revealed that she did have eyebrows once! However, it is believed that they either faded over time or were erased due to all the restoration work the portrait has undergone through the centuries.

She smiles (or does she?)

Another highly debatable fact regarding the portrait is whether or not Mona Lisa is smiling. Many artists and historians have provided their two cents on the topic. However, in 2000, a neuroscientist from Harvard, Dr. Margaret Livingstone, studied the painting and came up with a scientific explanation of the "optical illusion" that people are seeing in different ways. Livingstone's studies concluded that a smile (or the absence thereof) depends on one's frame of mind and focus at the time.

Letters to Lisa

Lady Lisa has been classified as a true heartbreaker, and many men are seduced by her quiet allure—so much so that they've done the strangest things "in the name of love." When the portrait was first hung in the Louvre in 1815, men flocked to the painting, gazed into her eyes, and left poems, impassioned notes, and even flowers to her. Even though there are over a million artworks in the museum's collection, Mona Lisa received so many letters of adoration, she got her own mailbox. Eventually, some of the letters got so heated, it was decided that Lady Lisa needed police protection—because later, as fate would have it, the portrait was kidnapped (stolen).

Who Doesn't Like a "True" Ghost Story?

America is a place rife with paranormal stories. One ghost story enthusiast Brad Culp started an on-campus magazine while studying at the Miami University in Oxford. He simply couldn't wait to pen stories of another life. He was particularly invested in one paranormal story: *The Ghost of Oxford Milford Road.*

The legend goes that circa 1940, a young fellow was dating a young lady from a rural settlement in his hometown. Unfortunately, the girl's parents disapproved of the relationship, and they had to meet in secrecy at an undisclosed location. So, every night, when the girl's parents went to bed, she would sneak out of her house, and when she reached the site, she would flash the car's headlights three times. This signal would then cause the gentleman to approach her on his motorcycle.

Sadly, he made a too-sharp turn one night and was flung off his steely steed. His injuries were grave, and he didn't survive. Apparently, he left this earth with unfinished business and is still haunting Milford Road in search of his lady love.

Culp, along with his girlfriend and another friend, headed out to Milford Road one night in search of the young man to verify the story. Brad's girlfriend was afraid she might panic and flee if they ran into the ghost. However, Culp was so inspired he thought he would use the opportunity to propose to his girlfriend. She didn't think much of the proposal but said yes nonetheless.

As Culp approached the lovers' undisclosed location, he decided to flash his car's headlights three times. And after a short time, they noticed a single headlight approaching the vehicle. The three occupants in the car got so freaked out that a collision might occur, they decided to switch the car's lights back on, and poof! The single headlight was gone!

They got out of the car to investigate but never found anything. So, if you're ever in the area and feeling nervy, why not simulate the events and experience them for yourself?

The President's Brain is Missing

President John F. Kennedy is not the only famous person whose brain went missing. Others include Galileo, Einstein, and even Beethoven. Is it too soon to say they are resting in pieces rather than peace?

The case of who stole Kennedy's missing brain has been boggling conspiracy theorists since 1966, after his assassination. The organ was removed during the autopsy, placed in a steel container with a screw-top lid, and stored in a filing cabinet of the Secret Service. Later, it was transported to a footlocker and held at the National Archives. It's said the footlocker in question was located in a secret room, along with other evidence from the assassination and the autopsy, but was later stolen. The discovery of the missing brain was made in October of 1966. The story goes that someone stole his brain because it would prove that he wasn't shot in the head by Lee Harvey Oswald on that fateful day.

The latest story that is doing the rounds is that none other than his brother Robert stole the brain, to preserve his honor. It's thought that President Kennedy was suffering from an unknown illness and took multiple prescription drugs to treat it—a fact that Robert wanted to keep hidden from the public. But like many other unexplained and unsolved mysteries, we'll probably never know (four decades later) what truly happened.

For centuries, the brain has been fascinating medical scholars—especially the brains of celebrities or those with outer-worldly talent. After Albert Einstein expired in 1955, his brain was removed during the autopsy for study purposes by Dr. Thomas Harvey (coincidence much?). Apparently, he dissected the genius's brain into one-hundred-odd slices, of which most are now missing.

In Galileo's case, sometimes missing body parts do turn up centuries later! In 2009, two of his digits and a tooth resurfaced. It's believed that these body parts were removed by some admirers and mysteriously disappeared for 95 years before making their way back to Florence at the Museum of the History of Science, which already had some of his other fingers in its custody.

Stop Smoking and Enter the Commonwealth Games

Steve Way was a bank worker, and in 2007, he smoked a 20-pack of ciggies a day, wore 38-inch pants, and totaled a weight of 231 lbs (104.78 kg). By the end of the year, he had had enough of his unhealthy lifestyle, and this made him change it for good!

He created the first stepping stone to health by quitting his smoking habit, giving up junk food, and picking up jogging. By 2008, his hard work paid off when he managed to run the London Marathon in 2:35, exceeding his own expectations of running it in under three hours.

Just two years later, in 2010, he completed his first marathon in under two hours and 20 minutes. In true fashion, the running bug had bitten him, and he continued to run his way to tougher races and longer distances.

As with all progress, he hit a spot where he became bored and stagnant and decided to shift his goal from running to being selected for the National British Commonwealth Athletic Team. In his last race leading to the road to the Commonwealth, he became the third-fastest Englishman in the 62.15 m (1000 km) category.

This saw him qualify for the Commonwealth Games at the age of 40. He finished 10th out of 27 runners. Moral of the story? Nothing is impossible.

Miss BumBum 2012 and the Witch Doctor Curse

In 2014, soccer star Cristiano Ronaldo had a really bad FIFA World Cup journey. One reason is that his home country of Portugal didn't even make it out of the group stages. Another reason is the runner-up of Miss BumBum Brazil 2012, who claimed to have fornicated with Ronaldo back in 2013.

Andressa Urach was obsessed with Cristiano and, under disguise, crashed one of Portugal's practices to get close to the soccer legend. She was very convincing and posed as a journalist for the *Muito Show*. She even boasted the required fake microphone and media credentials. She might've convinced others, but the security personnel spotted the intruder and removed her from the practice session immediately.

To add to the weirdness, Ronaldo experienced mysterious injuries during the World Cup. It was eventually diagnosed as a combination of tendinitis, an unexplained ache in his knee, and a muscle injury. Cristiano later said he was not in top form due to these medical conditions, but he didn't want to delve into specifics.

One Ghanaian witch doctor came forth to say that he had cursed the soccer star four months before the World Cup started. The curser, one Nana Kwaku Bonsam, told a radio station in Ghana that no medical treatment would cure Ronaldo's condition during the Big Daddy of soccer tournaments.

Even creepier, the Ghanaian witch doctor's name translates to the term "Devil of Wednesday." One can't help but wonder…

The Best Place to View Rainbows is in Hawaii

When it comes to viewing one of nature's most elusive and colorful natural occurrences, you'd need to look no further than the island of Hawaii. The two main components required to produce these beautiful phenomena are water and light. Due to this American state's endless supply of sunlight and water, it's rated at the top of the list when it comes to rainbows.

Hawaiian folklore states that rainbows represent "the veil between the realms of the gods and the realms of humans." And to boot, there are several different types of rainbows:

- Earth-clinging rainbows, called *uakoko*

- Barely-visible rainbows, called *punakea*

- Moonbows, called *ānuenue kau pō*

- Standing rainbow shifts, called *kāhili*

The occurrence of rainbows is common on our planet, but if you want to see some of the ones mentioned above or even a rainbow with a 360-degree circumference, you should come to the Rainbow State, a.k.a Hawaii.

There are many reasons why rainbows are rife in the Hawaiian archipelago and can even last for hours on end. The island's location in the subtropical Pacific makes it very susceptible to the influence of northeast tradewinds. These winds bring scattered rain showers and clear skies—the perfect recipe for rainbow chasing. Furthermore, the heat from the sea's surface, generated by the sunlight, radiates into the nighttime atmosphere.

Elvis Presley Sightings and Conspiracy Theories

The King of Rock and Roll died 45 years ago on August 16, 1977, but some are rubbishing these claims. Even though official medical reports state that he died of a heart attack in a bathroom of his Graceland mansion in Memphis, some die-hard fans (pun intended) are insisting that the crooner is still very much alive.

After his supposed death, many people have come forward to say that they have spotted the rock legend. Some of these far-fetched stories include:

First sighting after his death

A man claims to have seen Elvis shortly after the funeral. Apparently, this person was en route to a Memphis airport and bought a one-way ticket to Argentina when a man came over and introduced himself to the stranger as Jon Burrows. So, what is so significant about this name, you ask? Well, it was known that Presley often used it as an alias when making hotel reservations to preserve his true identity.

The "spelling error" on Elvis's headstone

On the gravestone where Presley is buried, his middle name is spelled "Aaron" instead of "Aron." Even though "Aaron" is his true middle name, it's believed that Elvis or his parents changed the spelling to honor his dead twin Jesse Garon Presley. Sadly Elvis's twin was stillborn at birth, and it's rumored that the spelling error was intentional and was the King's way of telling his fans that he isn't dead.

The intentional appearance in *Home Alone*

In the 1990 hit Christmas movie *Home Alone,* a boy is accidentally left behind while the rest of the family went on vacation. In one scene, the boy's mother can be seen desperately trying to get on a flight home so her son is not alone for Christmas. The movie was filmed 13 years after Elvis died, but one fan noticed a bearded man behind the mother at the ticket counter.

He looked to be about Presley's age (he would've been 55 in 1990), and his characteristics resembled many of Elvis's. For one, his eyes matched those of Presley, and in addition to the beard, the man had the style and natural coloring of the rock and roll legend. Elvis was born with blond hair but decided to dye his hair darker until the day he died.

Cloudy With a Chance of…

Weird weather patterns have been occurring for centuries, and the year 2021 was no exception. America was awash with phenomena like wildfires and low temperatures, but the most noteworthy came in Texas toward the end of the year when it rained fish!

The inhabitants of Texarkana thought they were reliving biblical times when they noticed a steady stream of fishes dropping from the heavens. This occurrence is actually called "animal rain" and has happened many times in the past, since 3rd-century AD. This strange event occurs when animals are scooped up by updrafts of water sprouts, making clouds of animals that are then deposited elsewhere by cruelly plummeting them to the ground in spectacular fashion.

The East Texas occurrence in particular only lasted a few minutes, but residents took to social media to share it with the world.

Where does the saying "raining cats and dogs come" from?

There are many ways in which we classify the amount of rain received during a rainfall, but one of the most commonly used terms has to be "it's raining cats and dogs." The person who introduced the term was Henry Vaughan, a British poet. In his

1651 book of poems, *Olor Iscanus*, the idiom was used to refer to a roof protection method against "dogs and cats rained in the shower."

By the 1710s, it had evolved into Jonathan Swift's poem *City Shower*, which included the term "raining cats and dogs" in reference to a heavy torrential downpour that left many animals dead in the streets. Swift had many other creative terms in his arsenal when referring to heavy rains, but it's the "cats and dogs" idiom that stuck and was eventually normalized by society.

The phrase is also believed to be a nod to Odin of Norse mythology, the God of Storms was regularly pictured with dogs. Dogs are the Norse symbol for wind, and black cats (synonymized with witches) later became the symbol for heavy rain in nautical terms. Hence the term "raining cats and dogs" was born, roughly translating to "a storm with wind and heavy rain."

The Greeks also have their own version of the story. The phrase *cata doxa* means "contrary to experience or belief," meaning the term is used as "you won't believe how hard it's raining."

1826's Eggnog Riot

Contrary to its world-class reputation today, West Point was seen completely differently somewhat 200 years ago. Then Colonel Sylvanus Thayer had extreme non-partying and non-drinking policies at this prestigious military school. Due to these outlandish rules, the West Point cadets of 1826 had the party of a lifetime, sans any liquor.

That year's year-end bash was different from others because it was the celebration of the 50th year of the school's existence, and the students were determined to make it an event to remember. They celebrated so hard that the party is forever etched in history as the "1826 Eggnog Riot."

As the Christmas countdown progressed, some students snuck in various types of alcohol such as brandy, rum, wine, and whiskey. They then combined all of these ingredients and concocted a homemade eggnog recipe for the party. Despite the booze stockpile, Christmas Eve came and went uneventfully until Captain Ethan Allen Hitchcock decided to go to bed. However, Colonel Thayer warned him that he suspected the students were planning a hoedown after the senior officers on duty turned in.

As Hitchcock slept, he was blissfully unaware of the chaos unfolding in the North Barracks—but by 4:00 a.m. Christmas morning, things had spiraled entirely out of control, causing Captain Hitchcock to wake from his sleep.

As he navigated his way through the hallways to get to the origin of the noise, he found a group of heavily drunk students and read them the riot act. Instead of the cadets heeding the warning from their superior, it had an adverse effect and angered them. Soon, they were seen throwing rocks through Hitchcock's bedroom window and even covering his door with wooden sticks. Some students went as far as carrying swords, muskets, and bayonets as their riot continued. Finally, one took it too far and started shooting at the captain. On Christmas morning, the violence and upheaval only came to a grinding halt at 6:05 a.m.

A little later that day, it soon became evident which of the students were involved in the debauchery from the previous evening. The cadets quartered in the South Barracks appeared well-rested and sober, while many of the students from the North Barracks were tremendously hungover. More than that was all the destroyed furniture, broken banisters, and shattered windows in the north wing.

It was later estimated that at least one-third of West Point's 260 students that year had engaged in the party. As a result, 22 of the offenders were slammed with house arrest on Boxing Day, with 19 being court-martialed later. All 19 students were found guilty, and 53 others faced less severe punishment. Since then, West Point cadets have thought twice before acting.

The World's Deepest River

Central Africa is host to one of the planet's largest and deepest rivers. The Congo River carries 1.25 million cubic feet of water, roughly the size of 12 Olympic-size swimming pools, into the Atlantic Ocean with every second that passes. This is more flow than any other river worldwide that is not located in the Amazon. But the most impressive fact of all is that the lower canyon of the Congo flows into the sea, creating what is known as the deepest river in the world. It's so deep that no one is really sure exactly how deep she runs.

As if the accolade of the world's deepest river isn't enough, there are many other fascinating facts around the Congo River, such as:

The fast currents proliferate evolution

It's a known fact that biologists are very fond of the lower Congo in particular. This is because it's the first place where they discovered animal populations that are divided by river currents. The river is less than a mile wide, but a new fish species has manifested on the two banks. This is due to the impenetrable currents that run through their environment. Today, we know that this small space of Earth boasts more unique species than any other place in the world.

The Congo River has no delta

All the ground deposits in the lower Congo washed out to create a very deep canyon-like structure located at the river's mouth. The majority of our other notable rivers end in a delta of creeks. However, the Congo flows in a narrow one-stream channel that scholars believe to be over 750 ft (0.22 km) deep in certain spots. To put this into perspective, it means that the channel holds sufficient water to submerge the MetLife Tower in Manhattan, America—and even have enough room for small fishing boats to pass over it.

Technically speaking, there are two Congo Rivers

If we travel to the top 2,500 mi (4023 km) of the Congo, we'll find one of the planet's laziest-flowing rivers that gently passes through the Central African continent and doesn't drop more than a foot per mile. Notably, the flow is relatively constant because it's so wide in length, and the Congo enjoys a bountiful rainy season right through the year.

Things You Didn't Know About Ancient Egypt

For these facts, we travel to Egypt, the place dubbed the "gift of the Nile." Apart from some of the stories we are all familiar with, there are some other surprising tales that have come from this biblical country.

It was the location of one of the first peace treaties ever to be signed

For nearly two centuries, the ancient Egyptians battled against the Hittite Empire in a showdown of control over what we call Syria today. Many bloody engagements took place, like the notable Battle of Kadesh in 1274 BC, but even when pharaoh Ramses II came into power, no victor had yet emerged. Both parties came under threat from other individuals, and this saw Ramses II and King Hattusili III come to a consensus in what we've come to know as the first peace treaty in history.

This agreement saw the conflict ending and both kingdoms concurring that they would back each other if any third party dared to interfere. This contract between Egypt and the Hittites is now known as the earliest surviving record of its kind and can be viewed at the entrance to the United Nations Security Council Chamber in New York.

Egyptians liked to play board games

With there being no TV and no social media in ancient Egypt, what did the inhabitants do for fun? Well, it's known that several different types of what we in modern times have come to know as board games were played. Some included Dogs and Jackals and Mehen, but the most notable has to be a game called Senet. Senet dates back to approximately 3500 BC and was played on an elongated board with 30 squares. Each player had a set of pieces that had to be moved along the board based on dice rolls or throwing sticks. The exact rules of Senet are still being speculated on by historians today, but one thing is for sure—it was very popular. The game can be seen in ancient Egyptian relics, like in a painting of Queen Nefertari playing Senet, and even King Tut had the board game buried with him in his tomb.

Taiwan's Liu Family Mansion

Constructed in 1929, the Baroque-style Minxiong ghost house—also called the Liu family mansion—has a terrible story to tell. It is located in the Chiayi countryside in the country's southwest region and has been abandoned since the 1950s, when the family fled its confines. Like all other unexplained stories, there are many theories around why the family fled their beautiful home so quickly.

Local lore speculates that the maid had an affair with Liu Rong-yu, her employer (the master of the house). When the wife discovered the secret affair, she is said to have made the worker's life so unbearable that she apparently jumped in the well (or was she pushed?). Then, she apparently came back from the dead to taunt the family, and this made them flee in fear.

Other suggested evidence that has come to light indicates that the house is haunted by soldiers from the Imperial Japanese Army. It is a known fact that a group of them were stationed at the mansion in WWII. One night, one of the soldiers saw a single figure roaming the grounds and raised the alarm by shooting at them. The rest of the cavalry woke and also opened fire. The next morning, all of the soldiers were inexplicably discovered dead, as it appeared they had shot at each other under cover of darkness.

But these are not the only two stories associated with this haunted house. In later years, certain members of the Kuomintang of China (KMT) occupied the place, and strangely enough, many of them died as a result of unexplained suicides, which only fueled speculations surrounding the hauntings. Many visitors claimed to have seen ghosts and experienced all sorts of paranormal occurrences.

The current owners of the land encourage visitors, but with a note of caution to stay clear of the well. The legend goes that if you are to get too close to the place where the Liu family maid met her demise, you'll end up with bad luck for the rest of your days on Earth. So, the only question left to ask is, do you dare?

True Stories About Famous Songs

What would we be without music? It's the essence of life itself, and no matter who you are, there are songs out there that bring us joy and even transport us to bittersweet memories.

Why "We Will Rock You" was written

The 1977 hit song that is still being played in sports stadiums worldwide to rouse crowds was the exact reason Freddy Mercury and Queen decided to write it. Guitarist Brian May recounts how the public responded to a particular phrase that Freddy coined years before—so much so that they decided to write a song where audience participation can be encouraged. And, as they say, the rest is history!

"Go Your Own Way"—literally!

It's only natural that when couples break up, some people feel the need to tell off the person who broke their heart. And the highly publicized and volatile relationship between Stevie Nicks and Lindsey Buckingham was no different. The popular song titled "Go Your Own Way" is said to be Buckingham's way of flipping the bird to ex Nicks after their breakup.

Dolly Parton's "I Will Always Love You"

When the queen of country's relationship with her mentor and duet partner, Porter Wagoner, ended in 1974, he had a tough time letting her go. So much so, in fact, that she wrote a song about it. This saw Wagoner eventually moving on as he realized there was no hope of rekindling a romance with Parton.

All of Billy Joel's Uptown Girls

It's no secret that singer Billy Joel dated a string of famous women. Many fans think that he penned the song "Uptown Girl" for model Christie Brinkley when they were dating. But later, Joel confessed that the song was, in fact, written for multiple high-profile women he had dated over the years, including Christie and Australian model/actress Elle Macpherson.

Who Turned Blake Shelton on?

Country crooner Blake Shelton's steamy hit song "Turnin' Me On" was written for none other than his current wife, Gwen Stefani. It's said that the lyrics "She's Revlon red in the blackest night" refer to the fact that she's Revlon's global ambassador and often wears red lipstick.

Conclusion

By now, you've learned many new facts and mind-blowing stories after reading this book. Hopefully you've enjoyed learning about these individuals and occurrences, and the intricacies that surround their tales.

You should be armed with many new facts and stories to tell your friends at school or share with your mates at the next gathering. This can even serve as a guide filled with new information to use before pub quiz events, or can be used by facilitators for trivia questions. Here's betting you didn't know about many of these facts—whether they were fascinating, out of this world, or just plain scary, there is no denying that they are an assault on the senses nonetheless!

Would you please be so kind as to leave a rating with your thoughts on the book? Any constructive criticism and feedback is welcomed that you deem necessary.

Dive Into...

THE
UNBELIEVABLE
FACTS
BOOK

Hilariously Weird Facts & Fascinating
Stories from Planet Earth

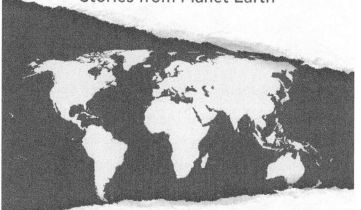

HENRY BENNETT

References

10 of the strangest animal stories from 2019. (n.d.).
Discover Wildlife.
https://www.discoverwildlife.com/animal-facts/strangest-
animal-stories-2019/

Agbatuka, C. (2015, July 4). *Jobless South African man
builds helicopter from recycled material.* Ventures
Africa. https://venturesafrica.com/jobless-south-african-
man-builds-helicopter-from-recycled-material/

Ali, R., & Amore, S. (2021, February 19). *17 times "The
Simpsons" predicted the future.* THEWRAP.
https://www.thewrap.com/simpsons-predicted-future-
gaga-nobel-disney-fox-hornets/

*All about Muang Boran, the world's Largest Open-Air
Museum.* (2022, January 21). Ripley's Believe It or Not!
https://www.ripleys.com/weird-news/all-about-muang-
boran-the-worlds-largest-open-air-museum/

Andrews, E. (2018a, August 29). *11 things you may not
know about ancient Egypt.* HISTORY.
https://www.history.com/news/11-things-you-may-not-
know-about-ancient-egypt

Andrews, E. (2018b, August 31). *10 little-known facts about Cleopatra*. HISTORY. https://www.history.com/news/10-little-known-facts-about-cleopatra

Ashmore, M. (2021, June 5). *Amelia Earhart's plane possibly found in Nikumaroro lagoon*. PR Newswire. https://www.prnewswire.com/news-releases/amelia-earharts-plane-possibly-found-in-nikumaroro-lagoon-301285325.html

Ballard, J. (2020, June 23). *42 famous songs and the true stories behind them*. Good Housekeeping. https://www.goodhousekeeping.com/life/entertainment/g32368739/true-story-behind-famous-songs/?slide=12

Barnett, E. (2021, December 23). *The Eggnog Riot of 1826*. Ripley's Believe It or Not! https://www.ripleys.com/weird-news/the-eggnog-riot-of-1826/

Benwell, L. (2020, July 26). *Deep Blue Sea 3 (SDCC 2020 review)*. GeekRockTV.com. https://geekrocktv.wordpress.com/2020/07/26/sdcc-2020-panel-deep-blue-sea-3/

Blaustein, M. (2014, December 23). *The year's 10 craziest sports stories you've never heard of*. NEW

YORK POST. https://nypost.com/2014/12/23/the-10-craziest-sports-stories-of-2014-youve-never-heard-of/

Blumberg, J. (2007, October 23). *A brief history of the Salem Witch Trials*. Smithsonian. https://www.smithsonianmag.com/history/a-brief-history-of-the-salem-witch-trials-175162489/

Brewster, W. (2021, May 8). *Nine of the greatest conspiracy theories in music history*. Mixdown Magazine. https://mixdownmag.com.au/features/nine-of-the-greatest-conspiracy-theories-in-music-history-2/

Campbell, D. (2017, July 14). *Close but no cigar: How America failed to kill Fidel Castro*. The Guardian. https://www.theguardian.com/world/2016/nov/26/fidel-castro-cia-cigar-assasination-attempts

Cane, T. (2021, October 5). *The stories behind the most mysterious places in the world*. Reader's Digest. https://www.rd.com/list/most-mysterious-places-in-the-world/

Captain Morgan. (n.d.). Diageo. https://www.diageo.com/en/our-brands/brand-profiles/captain-morgan/

Captain Morgan rum's sales volume United States, 2020. (n.d.). Statista.

https://www.statista.com/statistics/462661/captain-morgan-rum-us-sales-volume/

Castleton, D. (2021, July 21). *The monstrous & terrifying wild pigs of Hampstead's sewers*. David Castleton. https://www.davidcastleton.net/hampstead-wild-pigs-sewers-london-great-stink-queen-rat-bazalgette/

Chamary, J. V. (2020, June 30). *How genetic genealogy helped catch The Golden State Killer*. Forbes. https://www.forbes.com/sites/jvchamary/2020/06/30/gene tic-genealogy-golden-state-killer/?sh=1b0e75365a6d

Chavezbush, L. (2018, December 5). *The festival that honors monkeys with an epic banquet*. Atlas Obscura. https://www.atlasobscura.com/foods/monkey-buffet-festival

Christian, J. (2018, September 26). *Spotify will make a playlist based on your DNA*. Futurism. https://futurism.com/neoscope/spotify-playlist-dna

Cofield, C. (2016, February 22). *"Music" heard by Apollo 10 astronauts at the moon not from aliens*. SPACE. https://www.space.com/32007-alien-moon-music-apollo-10-explained.html

Cunningham, J. M. (2019). Howard Carter | British archaeologist. In *Encyclopedia Britannica*. https://www.britannica.com/biography/Howard-Carter

Daly, R. (2018, December 19). *Have we got music news for you: The 25 strangest NME stories of 2018*. NME. https://www.nme.com/blogs/nme-blogs/the-25-strangest-weirdest-music-news-stories-of-2018-2422632

De Maria, M. (2020, November 17). *30 Coca-Cola secrets you never knew*. Eat This, Not That! https://www.eatthis.com/coca-cola-facts/

Delzo, J. (2018, March 8). *Bones once thought to be a man's may belong to Amelia Earhart, scientist reveals*. Newsweek. https://www.newsweek.com/amelia-earhart-bones-man-837454

Did Vlad the Impaler drink blood? (2021). Study.com. https://study.com/academy/answer/did-vlad-the-impaler-drink-blood.html

Dimengo, N. (2014, May 29). *Athletes who bite*. Bleacher Report. https://bleacherreport.com/articles/2077716-athletes-who-bite

Docevski, B. (2017, December 8). *The Moberly–Jourdain incident: In 1901, two female academics claimed to have experienced a timeslip into pre-revolutionary France.*

The VINTAGE NEWS.
https://www.thevintagenews.com/2017/12/08/versailles-time-slip/

Dunlap, K. (2009, November 18). *NFL bans the Captain Morgan pose*. FindLaw.
https://www.findlaw.com/legalblogs/tarnished-twenty/nfl-bans-the-captain-morgan-pose/

Durian fruit - smelly, but also incredibly nutritious. (2016). Healthline.
https://www.healthline.com/nutrition/durian-fruit

Fahmy, M. (2007, November 26). Thailand lays on five-star buffet fit for monkeys. *Reuters*.
https://www.reuters.com/article/us-thailand-monkeys-idUSSP17762220071126

Foley, K. (n.d.). *Scarabs*. JHU Archaeological Museum.
https://archaeologicalmuseum.jhu.edu/staff-projects/ancient-egyptian-amulets/scarabs/

Frank Epperson. (2019). Massachusetts Institute of Technology. https://lemelson.mit.edu/resources/frank-epperson

Gaines, C. (2018, June 15). *Here are all 3 times Luis Suarez has bitten opponents*. INSIDER.
https://www.businessinsider.com/luis-suarez-biting-

151

history-2014-6?IR=T#that-last-one-left-a-visible-bite-mark-4

Gallagher, S. (2020, September 26). *Grease: Sandy Is Dead All Along (The Musical Is Just A Fantasy) - Theory Explained*. SCREENRANT. https://screenrant.com/grease-movie-sandy-dead-theory-explained/

Gamillo, E. (2021, March 25). *Hawai'i is officially the best place on Earth to see rainbows, according to science*. Smithsonian Magazine. https://www.smithsonianmag.com/smart-news/hawaii-best-place-earth-view-rainbows-heres-why-180977327/

Godfrey, A. (2015, January 30). *A golden shining moment: The true story behind Atari's ET, the worst video game ever*. The Guardian. https://www.theguardian.com/film/2015/jan/30/a-golden-shining-moment-the-true-story-behind-et-the-worst-video-game-ever

Goldman, A. L. (2002, June 29). Choi Hong Hi, 83, Korean general who created Tae Kwon Do. *The New York Times*. https://www.nytimes.com/2002/06/29/sports/choi-hong-hi-83-korean-general-who-created-tae-kwon-do.html

Groom, C. (n.d.). *Pepsi-Cola hits the spot*. Blogs@vt Sites. Retrieved December 29, 2021, from https://blogs.lt.vt.edu/cgrooms5/2016/02/14/pepsi-cola-hits-the-spot/

Hansen, E. (n.d.). *The English Civil Wars from 1642 to 1651*. The Classroom. https://www.theclassroom.com/english-civil-wars-1642-1651-23317.html

Hawkins, E. (2021, June 23). *A London influencer says she was abducted by aliens — and now is in love with one of them*. All That's Interesting. https://allthatsinteresting.com/abbie-bela

Hiskey, D. (2012, November 19). *When Julius Caesar was kidnapped by pirates, he demanded they increase his ransom*. MENTAL FLOSS. https://www.mentalfloss.com/article/13089/when-julius-caesar-was-kidnapped-pirates-he-demanded-they-increase-his-ransom

Homer, A. (n.d.). *What is the Oak Island Money Pit?* HISTORY. https://www.history.com/shows/the-curse-of-oak-island/articles/what-is-the-money-pit

Hornyak, T. (n.d.). *Shinjuku Station history – Shinjuku Station*. SHINJUKU STATION.

https://www.shinjukustation.com/shinjuku-station-history/

Ilic, J. (2021, February 22). *On this day: Roger Federer and Andre Agassi play on Burj Al Arab helipad*. Tennis World USA. https://www.tennisworldusa.org/tennis/news/Roger_Federer/95322/on-this-day-roger-federer-and-andre-agassi-play-on-burj-al-arab-helipad/

Jabbar, N. (2021, November 19). *Luis Suarez's bite on Otman Bakkal is even more shocking than the Branislav Ivanovic clash*. SPORT BIBLE. https://www.sportbible.com/football/news-suarezs-bite-on-bakkal-is-even-more-shocking-than-ivanovic-clash-20211119

Jennings, K. (2015, September 28). *The odd thing about the world's deepest river*. Condé Nast Traveler. https://www.cntraveler.com/stories/2015-09-28/odd-thing-about-the-worlds-deepest-river-congo-africa

Jeon, H. (2020, February 26). *Some fans of "Titanic" think Jack Dawson was actually from the future*. GOOD HOUSEKEEPING. https://www.goodhousekeeping.com/life/entertainment/g30812634/fan-theories-famous-movies/?slide=6

Joseph, A. (2021, November 18). *World's most expensive pigeon is worth INR 10.522 Crores*. Krishijagran. https://krishijagran.com/news/world-s-most-expensive-pigeon-is-worth-inr-10522-crores/

Jurberg, A. (2020, August 3). *Pepsi: The world's 6th largest military force*. Medium. https://bettermarketing.pub/pepsi-the-worlds-6th-largest-military-force-1388c488da8

Kamal, S. (2021, December 6). *When Roger Federer and Andre Agassi agreed to play on the world's deadliest tennis court in Dubai*. Www.sportskeeda.com. https://www.sportskeeda.com/tennis/news-why-roger-federer-andre-agassi-agreed-play-world-s-deadliest-tennis-court

Klein, C. (2015, December 22). *When Massachusetts banned Christmas*. HISTORY. https://www.history.com/news/when-massachusetts-banned-christmas

Lallanilla, M. (2017, September 14). *The real Dracula: Vlad the Impaler*. LIVESCIENCE. https://www.livescience.com/40843-real-dracula-vlad-the-impaler.html

Lethbridge, T. (2018, June 18). *Why people used to believe that ketchup was the cure for everything*. Twisted

Food. https://twistedfood.co.uk/why-people-used-to-believe-that-ketchup-was-the-cure-for-everything

Loeffler, J. (2020, February 5). *This Italian woman has been growing "eyelash-like" hairs from the gums in her mouth for years now.* All That's Interesting. https://allthatsinteresting.com/gingival-hirsutism

Lohnes, K. (2019). Dracula | Summary, characters, & facts. In *Encyclopedia Britannica.* https://www.britannica.com/topic/Dracula-novel

Lombard, S. (2020). *Tarantella: An Italian folk dance.* THE PROUD ITALIAN. https://theprouditalian.com/tarantella-an-italian-folk-dance/

Mark. (2018, May 31). *Abandoned Taiwan: The old Liu family mansion at Minxiong.* Kathmandu & Beyond. https://www.kathmanduandbeyond.com/abandoned-taiwan-old-liu-family-mansion-minxiong/

Mason, E. (2018, July 24). *8 things you (probably) didn't know about Tutankhamun.* HISTORY EXTRA. https://www.historyextra.com/period/ancient-egypt/8-things-you-probably-didnt-know-about-tutankhamun/

Mediratta, S. (2017, February 17). *Tomato ketchup was once sold as a medicine.* Inshorts.

https://inshorts.com/en/news/tomato-ketchup-was-once-sold-as-a-medicine-1487850469245

Mercy Brown and a New England vampire panic. (n.d.). Nightly Spirits. https://nightlyspirits.com/mercy-brown-and-a-vampire-panic/

Mylrea, H. (2019, January 2). *Elvis ain't dead – the weirdest Elvis Presley sightings and conspiracy theories.* NME. https://www.nme.com/blogs/nme-blogs/weirdest-elvis-presley-sightings-conspiracy-2125270-2125270

Nast, C. (2013, October 21). *Did RFK steal JFK's brain?* VANITY FAIR. https://www.vanityfair.com/news/2013/10/did-rfk-steal-jfk-s-brain

Nielsen, M. (2016, June 15). *These are the most popular alcoholic drinks in every state in the US*. SPOON UNIVERSITY. https://spoonuniversity.com/news/heres-the-alcoholic-drink-of-choice-in-all-50-states

Nigam, A. (2021, July 9). *Prince Charles, Camilla's self-proclaimed "love child" shares new comparison photos.* REPUBLICWORLD. https://www.republicworld.com/world-news/australia/prince-charles-camillas-self-proclaimed-love-child-shares-new-comparison-photos.html

Nolen, J. L. (2019). Bram Stoker | Irish writer. In *Encyclopedia Britannica.*
https://www.britannica.com/biography/Bram-Stoker

Oakes, K. (2017, July 10). *6 weirdly gripping space stories that are actually true.* BuzzFeed.
https://www.buzzfeed.com/kellyoakes/weird-but-true-space-stories

Offering the Presidency of Israel to Albert Einstein. (2019). Jewish Virtual Library.
https://www.jewishvirtuallibrary.org/offering-the-presidency-of-israel-to-albert-einstein

Patowary, K. (2018). *The War of The Bucket.* AMUSINGPLANET.
https://www.amusingplanet.com/2018/09/the-war-of-bucket.html

Patterson, M. (2013, November 13). Anthony Watts gets 8-week ban for biting opponent's penis in rugby league match. *Bleacher Report.*
https://bleacherreport.com/articles/1769320-rugby-league-star-gets-eight-week-ban-for-biting-opponents-penis-during-match

Peters, L. (2017, November 22). *7 stories of people who have claimed to travel in time.* Bustle.

https://www.bustle.com/p/7-stories-of-people-who-have-claimed-to-travel-in-time-5542920

Potter, N. (2012, February 20). *Flowering plant revived after 30,000 years in Russian permafrost*. Abc NEWS. https://abcnews.go.com/blogs/technology/2012/02/flowering-plant-revived-after-30000-years-in-russian-permafrost

Pruitt, S. (2018, August 23). *What happened to the Mary Celeste?* HISTORY. https://www.history.com/news/what-happened-to-the-mary-celeste

Puchko, K. (2015, April). *14 things you didn't know about the Mona Lisa*. MENTAL FLOSS. https://www.mentalfloss.com/article/62280/14-things-you-didnt-know-about-mona-lisa

Raj, R. (2016, July 8). *Coke was the 1st soft drink consumed in space*. Inshorts. https://inshorts.com/en/news/coke-was-the-1st-soft-drink-consumed-in-space-1467986068525

Reilly, L. (2013, June 26). *The time Napoleon was attacked by rabbits*. MENTAL FLOSS. https://www.mentalfloss.com/article/51364/time-napoleon-was-attacked-rabbits

Rohter, L. (2007, July 8). A huge Amazon monster is only a myth. Or is it? *The New York Times*. https://www.nytimes.com/2007/07/08/world/americas/08 amazon.html

Rowley, J. (2020, December 16). *Weird historical stories that sound made up (but aren't)*. Ranker. https://www.ranker.com/list/historical-weird-true-stories/jim-rowley

Saner, E. (2013, October 21). The president's brain is missing and other mysteriously mislaid body parts. *The Guardian*. https://www.theguardian.com/world/shortcuts/2013/oct/2 1/presidents-brain-missing-mislaid-body-parts

Santa Cruz del Islote, the most crowded Island in the world. (n.d.). Mybestplace. https://mybestplace.com/en/article/santa-cruz-del-islote-the-most-crowded-island-in-the-world

Scientists investigate how Arctic plant was brought back to life after 32,000 years. (2020, July 1). Sky News. https://news.sky.com/story/scientists-investigate-how-arctic-plant-was-brought-back-to-life-after-32-000-years-12018499

Shaquille O'Neal adds fuel conspiracy theory after claiming Stevie Wonder "saw" him in an elevator. (2019,

December 14). NZ Herald.
https://www.nzherald.co.nz/sport/shaquille-oneal-adds-
fuel-conspiracy-theory-after-claiming-stevie-wonder-
saw-him-in-an-
elevator/CMPOWM2YHEHOHDRO43JX2XX2LA/

Shilton, A. (2020, May 10). *3 true ghost stories for your
next backyard campfire*. Outside Online.
https://www.outsideonline.com/culture/essays-
culture/real-ghost-stories-for-campfires/

Simon, M. (2015, July 1). *Fantastically wrong: That time
people thought a comet would gas us all to death*.
WIRED. https://www.wired.com/2015/01/fantastically-
wrong-halleys-comet/

Smith, A. (2016, November 28). *Fidel Castro: The CIA's
7 most bizarre assassination attempts*. NBC News.
https://www.nbcnews.com/storyline/fidel-castros-
death/fidel-castro-cia-s-7-most-bizarre-assassination-
attempts-n688951

South African 10 babies story not true, inquiry finds.
(2021, June 23). *BBC News*.
https://www.bbc.com/news/world-africa-57581054

Springer, K. (2019, August 26). *The story behind
Vietnam's "Crazy House."* CNN.

https://edition.cnn.com/travel/article/crazy-house-dalat-vietnam/index.html

Talent converter. (n.d.). Julian Spriggs. https://www.julianspriggs.co.uk/pages/TalentConverter

Tapalaga, A. (2021, July 12). *Why did Albert Einstein refuse to become President?* Medium. https://historyofyesterday.com/why-did-albert-einstein-refuse-to-become-president-bfa5c5a5a7b2

Telusma, B. (2019, December 13). *Lionel Richie jokes he doesn't believe Stevie Wonder is blind.* TheGrio. https://thegrio.com/2019/12/13/say-what-lionel-richie-is-convinced-stevie-wonder-can-see/

The world's busiest train stations. (2012, August 8). RAILWAY TECHNOLOGY. https://www.railway-technology.com/features/featureworlds-busiest-train-stations/

TodayTix. (2017, April 19). *These Shakespeare conspiracies will blow your mind.* TodayTix. https://www.todaytix.com/insider/nyc/posts/these-shakespeare-conspiracies-will-blow-your-mind

Trosper, J. (2013, October 12). *10 mummies with mysterious stories to tell.* LISTVERSE.

https://listverse.com/2013/10/12/10-mummies-with-mysterious-stories-to-tell/

Walbank, F. W. (2019). Plutarch | Biography, works, & facts. In *Encyclopedia Britannica*. https://www.britannica.com/biography/Plutarch

Wansley, J. (2011, December 8). *Coca-Cola moves its secret formula*. World of Coca-Cola. https://www.worldofcoca-cola.com/media-alert/coca-cola-moves-its-secret-formula/

Waxman, O. B. (2017, April 8). *The bear who became a cigarette-smoking, beer-drinking World War II hero*. TIME. https://time.com/4731787/wojtek-the-bear-history/

Wayne, T. (2019). *PressReader.com - Connecting people through news*. Pressreader. https://www.pressreader.com/

Which year and era was the shortest war in history fought? (2021). Quora. https://www.quora.com/Which-year-and-era-was-the-shortest-war-in-history-fought?top_ans=323754586

Who invented the telephone? Antonio Meucci? (2022, January 3). The Proud Italian. https://theprouditalian.com/who-invented-the-telephone-antonio-meucci/

World facts - 50 interesting facts about the world. (2019, November 8). BESTLIFE. https://bestlifeonline.com/world-facts/

Yani, M. (2022, January 7). *Rare phenomenon makes it rain fish on Texas.* Ripley's Believe It or Not! https://www.ripleys.com/weird-news/rare-phenomenon-makes-it-rain-fish-on-texas/

Printed in Great Britain
by Amazon

79424114R00103